SHIPPING:

A SURVEY OF
HISTORICAL RECORDS

SHIPPING:
A SURVEY OF HISTORICAL RECORDS

edited by

P. Mathias
THE BUSINESS ARCHIVES COUNCIL

and

A. W. H. Pearsall
THE NATIONAL MARITIME MUSEUM

DAVID & CHARLES : NEWTON ABBOT

ISBN 0 7153 5384 5

Typeset by The Western Litho Company (Plymouth) Limited
Printed in Great Britain by Redwood Press Limited Trowbridge Wilts
for David & Charles (Publishers) Limited
South Devon House Newton Abbot Devon

CONTENTS

The Business Archives Council has been concerned for some years with instituting surveys of the historical records of various branches of enterprise. The first section of the present check list — records of shipping companies — is the first of such surveys to appear. A survey of the historical records of British banks, as the second venture, has now been launched. The main initial work of the council, following its formation in 1934, was to produce a general register of business archives held by those firms who replied to a questionnaire. This large register still exists, although now suffering from the attrition (of firms and records) brought by war and post-war hazards.

Since then the situation concerning the preservation of business records has changed considerably. On the credit side is the fact that county archivists are now very much more actively concerned with business records than before the war. The National Register of Archives lists such accessions systematically and its staff actively aid the search for new material. Under the spur of coping with the flood of contemporary material rather than just out of concern with their ancient records, many more firms have themselves appointed professional archivists, who have brought new standards to the preservation and maintenance of these categories of documents. More economic historians in more universities and colleges are concerned to use business records, and to help their preservation. Against these advantages still work the ancient enemies of neglect and ignorance; lack of knowledge being more insidious than deliberate ill-will. The spate of mergers sweeping across many branches of industry has created an increasing hazard. And, paradoxically, so has the tardy recognition of the value of important collections of business documents. There is now a much higher incentive to put collections under the hammer, a financial advantage which sometimes leads to the break-up of collections and their dispersal amongst large numbers of private buyers by auction-

ing individual documents in separate lots. American collectors
— individuals, universities and libraries — have larger purses
than most British depositories so that the risk of exports must
rise in the future, particularly in the absence of any effective
restraining legislation.

The increasing complexity of recording known business
archives, and the continuous accretion of records, means that
the general national survey, conducted by questionnaire, is
no longer a practical proposition. A systematic national
search, conducted by a team of professionally trained
archivists, would demand enormous resources. In the
circumstances the council feels that a series of industry
surveys has a better chance of success. By concentrating on a
narrower front, hopefully the coverage can be more systematic
and the expense (both of producing the survey and of
subsequently publishing it) more manageable. Although the
present check-list of shipping company records has inevitably
suffered from facing many difficulties for the first time, the
council hopes that its appearance will prove of importance to
scholars concerned with the history of shipping and an
encouragement which may make it possible to augment the
coverage of the list on a future occasion.

The questionnaire sent by the council to shipping companies
proved exactly complementary to one sent to record offices
by the National Maritime Museum at Greenwich. The
resulting replies form a happy marriage in the two sections of
this publication.

It is the museum's policy vigorously to seek to encourage
the preservation of merchant shipping records. To this end,
besides the current survey, it is collaborating with the Public
Record Office, the Board of Custom and Excise, and with
Lloyd's Register of Shipping and other institutions, both in
the preservation of material and in making it more accessible
to students. In particular, the museum is seeking to build up
a central transcript of all material available as the result of

the vessel registration requirements of the successive Merchant Shipping Acts. The museum is also conducting a survey, based on interview and questionnaire, into conditions of service in the merchant shipping industry at sea in the early years of the present century.

Peter Mathias, Chairman,
Business Archives Council

Chichele Professor of Economic History,
University of Oxford

Basil Greenhill, Director,
National Maritime Museum Greenwich,
London, SE10

ACKNOWLEDGEMENTS

The Business Archives Council owes a debt of gratitude to many individuals and institutions for help in the preparation and publication of this book. The late Lord Twining and Commander Douglas Doble, as the then chairman and secretary of the council, were instrumental in organising the survey, and Commander Doble subsequently did much work on the preparation of the manuscript. Sir Nicholas Cayzer, Bt, chairmen of the British and Commonwealth Shipping Co Ltd, now happily a vice-president of the council, wrote to the chairman of fourteen leading shipping companies seeking their participation in the survey. Also, through his initiative, Anchor Line Limited, Bibby Line Limited, Blue Funnel Line Limited, Bolton Steam Shipping Co Limited, Bowater Steamship Co Limited, Coast Lines Limited, Wm Cory & Son Limited, Furness Withy & Co Limited, H. Hogarth & Sons Limited, Glen Line Limited, Houlder Brothers & Co Limited and P & O Lines made a loan towards the cost of the survey and its publication. To all of these companies, to the City of Bristol (which also made a grant) and to all those agreeing to list records the council offers its grateful thanks.

Many other individuals have been generous in the time they have given to the survey. Mr R. Craig of University College, London listed the records of Royal Mail now in the library of University College and checked other details. Professor F.E. Hyde, Dr J.R. Harris and Dr P. Davies of Liverpool University, and Mr B. Redwood, County Archivist of Cheshire, gave similar help. Mrs Mann at Ormand House did much of the typing and Dr A. Keep meticulously transcribed, standardised and collated all the data from the questionnaires. To all these persons the council offers its thanks.

The National Maritime Museum is also grateful to Mr R. Craig and to all those archivists who responded to its request for information about relevant material within their care.

The survey of shipping company records which follows is far from complete (as may be surmised from a total number of extant firms of over 700 compared with the 35 principal entries in the list). However, many archives have disappeared without trace, with war-time destruction, salvage drives, mergers, neglect, and the problems of space in the ever more valuable storage area at head offices. Doubtless more records will come to light, perhaps their existence being reported as a result of the appearance of this check list. As this goes to be printed there is a hope that further Cunard material may be recovered in Liverpool. Shortage of time and resources prevented all the documents reported from being professionally checked. Doubtless, therefore, corrections will need to be made for some of the items printed in Section I. Needless to say, any emendations of, or supplementations to, the entries will be gratefully received by the council.

Section I is published, not as a comprehensive and authoritative calendar of the records of shipping companies, but with the more modest aim of reporting the existence of important new archive material, part of the historical heritage of the British economy. Brief histories of the shipping lines, details of mergers and subsidiary companies are given in support of the documents.

The second part of this survey began with a questionnaire sent out by the National Maritime Museum in 1967 to all record offices in the United Kingdom with a view to maintaining a central record of maritime records in more detail than could the National Registry of Archives. The museum subsequently became aware of the widespread need for guidance in locating records of merchant shipping in particular, and the intentions of the Business Archives Council fitted in very well with those of the museum. Knowledge of additional material in this Section will also be welcomed.

The books mentioned in the first section are not intended

to form a comprehensive bibliography. They are confined to substantial and readily obtainable works relating specifically to the entries concerned. Many of the numerous company histories in pamphlet form, often privately printed, will feature in a section of the National Maritime Museum's Library catalogue, to be published, it is hoped, in the early 1970s.

It should also be stressed that important historical material about shipping in the public records is not included, such as the customs and excise collections (both in the Public Record Office and in the archive deposit at the Customs and Excise), the Port Books, State Papers, domestic Chancery records, Court of Bankruptcy, Courts of Admiralty, the Register of Shipping, the logs of vessels on charter to the East India Company which are in the India Office Library, the Lloyds Survey Reports and other material in the National Maritime Museum. Insurance records provide another large treasure-house for shipping material, and the successive volumes of Lloyds Register of Shipping (now in course of reprinting) are on deposit at the Guildhall Library, London. There is also an almost complete set at Greenwich. A comprehensive bibliography of shipping items (both books and articles in periodicals) is in the early stages of preparation in the National Maritime Museum. A published international bibliography, now in several parts, has been edited by Professor R.G. Albion, of Harvard University and another of material published in this century is in preparation under the auspices of the International Commission for Maritime History. Further information about the existence of particular manuscript material may be located through the subject index of the National Register of Archives at Quality House, Quality Court, Chancery Lane, London, WC1. This includes numerous references to maritime matters, records of individual ships, bills of sale, shippers' correspondence and accounts, and material relating to docks, harbours, seamen, etc. These references are additional to the main groups of papers recorded in the annual lists of the NRA *Sources of Business History in the National Register of Archives.*

Material from various shipping businesses has also been deposited at the Institute of Chartered Shipbrokers in London. Other papers preserved at the institute include schemes of freight controls (mainly from the 1930s) and a very large collection of charter-parties, dating from the early years of this century, covering most deep-sea trades of the world. Known papers of shipping companies involved in Latin-American trade are listed in D.C.M. Platt (ed), *Latin-American Business Archives in the United Kingdom* (1965), pp 83–8.

SECTION I

SHIPPING COMPANIES

1 HISTORY

This great name in Scottish shipping first appears in 1856, when the Anchor Line of steam packet ships opened a service between Glasgow and New York with the sailing of the steamer *Tempest* under the operation of the firm of Handyside & Henderson. Captain Thomas Henderson, one of four brothers who, like their father, were all master mariners, was the driving force behind the Anchor Line. By 1866 the New York service had developed into a weekly sailing, and from 1868 a service was started between Scandinavian ports and Leith bringing emigrants who were taken by rail to Glasgow. A service was also started between London and New York and between London and Boston. These lasted from about 1876 until 1881, when they were given up in favour of a service between Glasgow and Calcutta, which carried on for thirty years until Anchor Line sold their Calcutta conference rights to Brocklebanks.

In 1863 the Anchor Line of Peninsular & Mediterranean Steam Packets was formed to take over the line between Glasgow and Lisbon. This service was soon extended to take in Spain, Italy and Sicily, and by 1866 a monthly service to Egypt. The opening of the Suez Canal in 1869 led to the start of a Bombay service. This service, together with the Atlantic services out of Glasgow and Naples, was being operated when war broke out in 1914. At that date the company owned thirteen ships totalling 86,746 tons; of these seven were sunk by enemy action.

Immediately after the war a building programme was put into operation, but it was decided to withdraw from the Italian service to New York in the face of increasing competition from Italian ships, so that of all the trades the company had engaged in for long or short periods, only the New York and Bombay services survived. These continued to take both passengers and cargo.

The years between the two world wars proved increasingly difficult as a result of the world-wide trade depression, on top of which, in September 1930, the United States announced the suspension of all but non-quota visas. This especially affected the Anchor Line as its westbound traffic depended largely on Scottish emigrants. As time went on, trade conditions grew still worse and in April 1935 Anchor Line (Henderson Brothers) Ltd went into liquidation. The assets were transferred to a new company, Anchor Line (1935) Limited, under the chairmanship of Lord Runciman, with the whole of the ordinary shares and debentures owned by a syndicate formed by Dawnay Day & Co Ltd. Runciman (London) Ltd were appointed managers. Shortly afterwards the date '1935' was dropped from the title.

The two services to New York and to Bombay continued to be operated and plans were launched to recondition the Atlantic ships and to build new tonnage for the Indian service. By 1938 the scheme for the Atlantic ships was completed and two motor passenger ships had been built for the Indian route. During the war several Anchor liners were requisitioned for service as armed merchant cruisers and others carried out various duties for which they were more suited. Six ships were lost by enemy action including most of the famous Atlantic passenger ships. Conditions after the war did not warrant their replacement and the character of the New York service was changed, three cargo/passenger ships each carrying twelve passengers being employed. In 1956 these ships were transferred to the Bombay service and the Atlantic was served by three cargo ships.

In 1949 the United Molasses Company obtained a controlling interest, ultimately acquiring the entire capital four years later.

In 1965 the decision was taken to give up the passenger service to Bombay and in the same year the company was purchased by Moor Line of Newcastle.

2 PRESENT STATUS AND ACTIVITIES

The company is a wholly owned subsidiary of Moor Line Ltd and runs two liner services, one to west coast ports of India and Pakistan and the other in association with Cunard Steamship Co Ltd to the east coast of the United States.

3 RECORDS HELD

Minute books from 1935
Day books from 1961
Purchases books from 1961
Cash books from 1961
Bill books from 1961
Ledgers from 1961
Legal records: management agreements from 1935; memorandum and articles of association from 1935; agency agreements from 1950; other agreements from 1936.
The records are in good condition.

4 ACCESS

Access is granted to approved students and portions of records may be temporarily removed. Enquiries may be addressed to the Company Secretary, Anchor Line Ltd, 59 Waterloo Street, Glasgow C 1, or to 52 Leadenhall Street, London EC3.

5 REFERENCE

McLellan, R.S. *Anchor Line 1856—1956* (Glasgow, Anchor Line 1956)

1 HISTORY
   See Coast Lines Ltd

2 PRESENT STATUS AND ACTIVITIES
   The company is a subsidiary of Coast Lines Ltd and runs
services between Liverpool and Belfast.

3 RECORDS HELD
   Day books from 1950 to 1966
   Sales books from 1962 to 1966
   Consignments from 1960 to 1966
   Cash books from 1950 to 1966
   Bill books from 1962 to 1966
   Ledgers from 1924 to 1966
   Other financial records from 1924 to 1966
   Stock or inventory books from 1948 to 1966
   Wages books from 1952 to 1966
   Legal records: agency agreements from 1950
   to 1966; employment agreements from 1950
   to 1966; documents relating to title from
   1824 to 1966.
The general records are kept at the Belfast office and the
secretarial records at the office of Coast Lines Ltd, London.

4 ACCESS
   Enquiries may be addressed to the Company Secretary,
Belfast Steamship Company Ltd, 42 Donegall Quay, Belfast 1.

5 REFERENCE
   Duckworth, C.L.D. and Langmuir, G.E.
Clyde and Other Coastal Steamers (Brown, Sue
& Ferguson 1939)
   McNeil, D.B. *Irish Passenger Steamship
Services,* vol 1, (Newton Abbot 1969)

1 HISTORY

Alexander and William Thomson set up a shipbrokers' business in Leith in 1825 and also imported marble. Alexander confined himself mainly to trading activities and William looked after the management of the ships. The financial support of two Alloa families, the Thomsons and the Mitchells, enabled the brothers to start a regular trade between Leith and Canada: coal outwards and timber inwards. In 1847 Alexander withdrew from active partnership and the name of the firm was changed to William Thomson & Co. The dependence on the Alloa families gradually diminished and William Thomson & Co came to be a substantial shipowning firm in its own right. Voyages further afield were undertaken, some on charter while others were independent trading ventures. Those to the Far East demonstrated the possibilities of trade in this area — a trade in which William Thomson & Co soon acquired a substantial interest.

The Canadian trade declined with the passing of the sailing ships and in its place grew up a subsidiary trade to the Baltic carried on in steamships. Expansion in size, numbers and activities continued until 1914. A regular berth service for the carriage of general cargoes to the Far East developed. As coal ceased to be the staple outward cargo, more of the ships loaded at London and less at Leith. The Baltic trade of the company was virtually ended by the 1914—18 war.

After the war single-ship accounting was abandoned and in 1919 Ben Line Steamers Ltd was formed to amalgamate all interests into the one company. Between the wars the company's fleet grew in size and numbers, and in 1943 the head office was transferred from Leith to Edinburgh. In the post-war period trade with Japan has been greatly increased.

The company established an office at Singapore and at London Docks in 1951, one at Port Swettenham in 1954, one at Kuala Lumpur in 1957, and offices at Hongkong and Bangkok in 1958.

2 PRESENT STATUS AND ACTIVITIES

The company is one of shipowners and managers whose activities are world-wide.

3 RECORDS HELD

The company's records are deposited in Edinburgh University Library.

The company holds records of Petrograd Steamers Ltd from 1921 to 1942, when this company was wound up.

4 ACCESS

Enquiries should be made to the Librarian, Edinburgh University Library.

5 REFERENCE

Blake, G. *The History of Wm Thomson and Co of Leith and Edinburgh, and of the Ships owned by them* (1956)

MacGregor, D.R. *The China Bird: the history of Captain Killick and one hundred years of Sail and Steam* (1961)

Milne, T.E. 'British Shipping in the 19th Century: A Study of the Ben Line ...' P. Payne (ed), *Studies in Scottish Business History* (Glasgow 1967)

Somner, G. *Ben Line Fleet List and Short History* World Ship Society Kendal (1967)

BOLTON STEAM SHIPPING COMPANY LTD

1 HISTORY

The company had its origin in 1884 when Mr (later Sir) Frederic Bolton, a marine underwriter and insurance broker at Lloyd's, decided to become a shipowner. Until 1895 the shipping business was run as a partnership, the partners being Mr Louis T. Bartholomew (1885—97) and later Mr Henry Kenneth (1887—97), but when the Bolton-Kenneth partnership was dissolved in 1895 the Bolton Steam Shipping Company was formed under the management of F. Bolton & Co, a partnership which owned the insurance interests. At the beginning of World War I the company owned seven ships, but by 1917 only four ships remained. Owing to increased ill health, the death of his elder son who had been closely associated with him in the business, and other difficulties, Sir Frederic sold the fleet and wound up the company in 1919. He died a year later.

In 1921 Sir Frederic's second son, Louis Hamilton Bolton, decided to revive the company. Three second-hand ships were bought and later that year a new ship which was under construction. These ships were replaced by newly built vessels in 1929—32. Like the earlier company, the new company was managed by F. Bolton & Co, and this arrangement continued until 1935 when the first board of directors of the Steam Shipping Company was appointed. When war broke out in 1939 the company owned three vessels and had two new ships on order. Two of the original vessels were lost with heavy casualties in 1942. Later that year the company bought the share capital of Glover Brothers, a firm of shipbrokers with whom it had been closely associated in business for sixty years. Glovers were originally shipowners themselves. At one time they had a financial interest in the Mercantile Shipping Company which they also managed and later were the sole owners of the Shakespear Shipping Company.

Excluding two ships bought from the government, the company ended the war as it had begun — with three vessels — and it therefore set about building up its fleet. Two 'Ocean' ships and an 'Empire' were bought but these, together with the two government ships, were sold in 1951 to enable the company to build new tonnage. In 1953 Mr L.H. Bolton died and his son Mr F.B. (Tim) Bolton became chairman of the firm. A year later, whilst continuing to manage its own fleet, the company branched out into a new management and part ownership venture — the North Yorkshire Shipping Company — which was formed in partnership with BISC (Ore) Ltd and Smith's Dock Company. Four iron-ore carriers were built to operate on long-term charters. By 1963 Boltons had acquired all the share capital in this company, which it continues to run today as a wholly owned subsidiary.

In 1965 all the Bolton shipping and insurance interests were grouped. The shipping company thus acquired the shares in its associated underwriting agency and brokerage companies. Later the same year the company diversified its interests by purchasing a 25 per cent holding in Transglobe Airways Ltd, an independent airline operating Britannia aircraft from Gatwick.

Traditionally Bolton ships have always been named after famous painters beginning with the letter 'R'. The exceptions are the iron-ore carriers which are named after places in North Yorkshire.

2 PRESENT STATUS AND ACTIVITIES

This company is one of shipowners. In addition to their other interests Boltons own seven ships, the largest a bulk carrier of 27,000 tons deadweight.

3 RECORDS HELD

Minute books from 1897
Consignments (12 vols of journals) from 1921
Cash books (20 vols) from 1921
Ledgers (25 vols) from 1921
Balance sheets for 1902, 1917, 1922–5, 1928, 1930–5
Share distribution list of 1897
Wages books (6 vols) for office staff and merchant naval personnel ashore from 1947 to 1966

Pension records of merchant naval officers
from 1937
Legal records: agreements from 1956
Letters: correspondence regarding ships,
masters, crew etc from 1956; general
correspondence from 1959; letters from Sir
Frederic Bolton, founder of the firm from
1881 to 1894
Miscellaneous: descriptions and photographs
of company's ships from 1885; officers'
register from 1895; ship's deck and engine
log books (approx 600) from 1952; voyage
statistics from 1904; voyage records (lists of
crew, wages etc) from 1939; meteorological
log of the *Reynolds* from 1898 to 1899.

4 ACCESS

Enquiries may be addressed to the Company Secretary,
The Bolton Steam Shipping Co Ltd, Ibex House, Minories,
London EC3.

BOOKER BROS (LIVERPOOL) LTD

1 HISTORY

Josiah Booker, a native of Lancashire, set foot in Demerara
(Guyana) in 1815 and became a sugar planter. Some of his
brothers joined him and established an office in Liverpool in
1832. Their first deep-sea ship traded out of Liverpool to
Demerara in 1835 and the Booker Line service has been
maintained ever since. John McConnell was also a Demerara
sugar planter. The two family businesses combined in 1870,
and in 1900 the name of the firm was changed to Booker
Bros McConnell & Co Ltd. The following firms became its

subsidiaries: Arakaka Steamship Co (1913), S. Wm Coe & Co Ltd (incorporating Thorn Line Ltd) (1955), and Booker Merchantmen Ltd.

2 PRESENT STATUS AND ACTIVITIES

The company is one of shipowners (deep sea and coastal) and has interests in sugar, shops, rum, printing, engineering, etc. Deep sea ships (Booker Line and Booker Merchantmen) trade with the West Indies and the coasters (Coe's) trade primarily with Northern Ireland. The subsidiary companies operate in the West Indies as shipowners, trawler owners, shipping and insurance agents, stevedores, wharf owners and bulk terminal operators. Business is conducted from Liverpool. The company acts as holding company for the shipping interests of Booker Bros McConnell & Co Ltd, Bucklersbury House, 83 Cannon Street, London EC4.

3 RECORDS HELD

Minute books from 1913 to 1967
Wages books from 1917 to 1967
Voyage profits (not detailed) of deep sea ships from 1887 to 1912
Legal records: a few old partnership agreements, deeds etc from the mid-nineteenth century, mostly concerning business in Guyana and with little reference to shipping.

The records are in a fair condition, unclassified, and not extensive. During World War II the Liverpool office was bombed and almost all records destroyed.

4 ACCESS

Enquiries may be addressed to the Company Secretary, Booker Bros (Liverpool) Ltd, Martins Bank Buildings, Water Street, Liverpool 2.

1 HISTORY

The Bowater Steamship Company was formed in 1955 as a wholly owned subsidiary of the Bowater Paper Corporation in order to serve its mills in the United Kingdom, United States of America, Canada and Europe and its selling companies in these areas and elsewhere. The ownership of a shipping line provides the company with an insurance against delays in obtaining chartered tonnage for the transportation of raw materials needed by their mills and for the delivery of their finished products overseas, and also against any undue rise in freight rates due to a shortage of charter ships, particularly in times of emergency.

Since 1938 when they took over the Corner Brook Mills in Newfoundland, Bowaters had owned two newsprint carriers, the SS *Corner Brook* and *Humber Arm*. These ships were used to deliver newsprint from the Corner Brook Mill to customers in the United States and elsewhere. The SS *Humber Arm* was lost during the war and the SS *Corner Brook* was disposed of after the war. In 1955 two new ships of some 6,500 gross registered tons each, were built in Scotland for the Bowater Steamship Co Ltd. These were the newsprint carriers *Margaret Bowater* and *Sarah Bowater*. Following these two vessels the company built seven more ships, namely the *Nicolas Bowater* (a newsprint carrier of 7,000 gross registered tons) and six pulp and pulpwood carriers (*Alice, Constance, Elizabeth, Gladys, Nina* and *Phyllis Bowater*) of 4,000 gross registered tons each.

The smaller vessels were so designed to enable them to enter the port of Risor in Norway, not then navigable by the larger vessels. In order that the pulp carriers might more safely negotiate the bends and narrows of the River Swale to Ridham in Kent they were fitted with Pleuger rudders. All these vessels were put into service between 1958 and 1961 and it was estimated they would carry between them about half the total tonnage of Bowater products each year.

Following the acquisition by the Bowater Paper Corporation of the Mersey Paper Co of Liverpool, Nova Scotia, which took place in 1956, four vessels operated by that company — *Vinland, Markland, Liverpool Rover* and *Liverpool Packet* — were taken over by a new company formed under the name of the Bowater Steamship Co of Canada Ltd. With the exception of the *Markland* these vessels were old, and the *Vinland* was sold in December 1959. In January 1960 the Bowater Steamship Co of Canada was wound up and the three remaining vessels were taken over by the Bowater Steamship Co of London. For two to three months in the year the port of Corner Brook (Newfoundland) is generally icebound and only ice-breakers can go in; to a lesser extent similar conditions obtain at Holmsund (Sweden) and Risor (Norway). The total fleet of twelve ships was therefore difficult to schedule satisfactorily to keep them all occupied. This fact, together with the age of two of them, decided the fate of the Canadian vessels, and by 1963 all three had been sold. The Bowater Steamship Co was thus left with the nine newest ships, all built since 1955.

Initially managed by the personnel of the Bowater Steamship Co Ltd, the day-to-day management of the Bowater fleet was contracted out to Cayzer, Irvine & Co Ltd in 1963.

2 PRESENT STATUS AND ACTIVITIES

The company is a wholly owned subsidiary of the Bowater Paper Corporation Ltd and its activities are therefore directed and limited according to the needs of this organisation. The company is one of shipowners and has a fleet of vessels carrying raw materials and finished paper for the companies of the Bowater organisation. Business is conducted in Canada (including Newfoundland), USA and Scandinavia. Vessels run on regular routes from Corner Brook and Liverpool, Nova Scotia, to American Atlantic coast ports, and from Corner Brook to the Great Lakes, with newsprint cargoes, and from

Newfoundland and Charleston, SC, and from Risor and
Holmsund to the UK with pulp cargoes.

3 RECORDS HELD

Minute books from 1955.
Legal records: important agreements,
apprenticeship indentures, employment
agreements.
Apprenticeship indentures and employment agreements are
kept by Cayzer Irvine & Co.
(The company was formed in 1955 and all important documents are therefore still of current importance rather than
as an archive.)

4 ACCESS

Enquiries may be addressed to the Bowater Paper
Corporation Ltd, Bowater House, Knightsbridge, London SW1.

THE BRISTOL CITY LINE OF STEAMSHIPS LTD

1 HISTORY

Founded in 1704, this appears to be the oldest shipping
firm in the world still engaged in the shipping business. The
founder, James Hillhouse, died in 1754. His son continued
his interest and the latter's son started to build ships. As
many as twenty ships were built from 1801 to 1820, many
of them warships for the Royal Navy in the Napoleonic
Wars, including the famous HMS *Arethusa*. Some ships were
also completely owned by the firm and of these it had fifteen
in 1825. From 1821 to 1850 no less than fifty ships were
built.

In 1836 the firm started the Bristol Steam Navigation Co.
Between 1851 and 1878 they owned and ran thirty-seven
sailing ships. In 1872 there were eighteen ships in the Blue
Star Fleet.

In 1879 the Bristol City Line of steamships was started which in 1900 possessed ten steamships. Between 1912 and 1951 as many as 240 ships were built.

In 1948 the Bristol City Line of Steamships Ltd bought the other connected firms and became the present company.

2 PRESENT STATUS AND ACTIVITIES

The company engages in all kinds of shipping business, including shipbuilding. Trade is carried on with Africa, the West Indies and North America.

3 RECORDS HELD

No details are recorded.

4 ACCESS

Enquiries may be addressed to Charles Hill of Bristol Ltd, 129 Cumberland Road, Bristol.

REFERENCE

Hill, J.C.G. 'Shipshape and Bristol Fashion', *Liverpool Journal of Commerce*, 1951.

THE BRISTOL STEAM NAVIGATION COMPANY LTD

1 HISTORY

The company was founded on 23 August 1836.

2 PRESENT STATUS AND ACTIVITIES

The company owns vessels and operates general cargo liner services. Trade is carried on between Plymouth, Bristol, Newport and Swansea in the UK, and Antwerp and Rotterdam; also between Bristol and Dublin.

3 RECORDS HELD

Minute books from 1924

Legal records: Deeds of Accession to Deed of
Settlement of the Bristol General Steam
Navigation Co dated 23 August 1836, with
signatures under seals of original shareholders.
Miscellaneous: handbills advertising sailings
to and from Bristol (1850, 1871).
Records are held for the Bristol General Steam Navigation Co.

4 ACCESS

Enquiries may be addressed to the company secretary.

5 REFERENCE

Farr, G. *West Country Passenger Steamers*
(Tilling, 1950).

THE BRITISH & COMMONWEALTH
SHIPPING COMPANY LTD

1 HISTORY

In 1900, Sir Donald Currie, the founder of the Castle Line,
joined forces with the Union Line to form Union-Castle, and
the Cayzer family, in 1956, merged their interests in Clan
Line Steamers with those of Union-Castle to form The British
& Commonwealth Shipping Co Ltd. In 1878 Charles Cayzer,
later Sir Charles Cayzer Bt, founded the Clan Line. His grandson, Sir Nicholas Cayzer Bt, is the present chairman of the
group. He and other members of the family take an active part
in the management of the group, which is controlled by
family interests. The business originated in the Union Collier
Co, established in 1853. By 1856 the collier business had been
abandoned and the name changed to the Union Steam Ship Co
Ltd. In the following year a contract was signed with the South
African Government for the provision of a mail service
between England and South Africa and the *Dane,* a ship of

500 tons, in that year inaugurated a service which continues to this day.

The Castle Line was founded in 1862, and ten years later entered the South African trade. From then until the merger in 1900 the fiercest rivalry existed between the Union and Castle Lines. Since then the company has maintained the South African mail service, probably the most regular and reliable ocean-going shipping service in the world, as well as other passenger and cargo services to South and East Africa. In 1858 the White Cross Line, later to become Bullard King & Co Ltd, began sailings to Natal and in the late eighties inaugurated a direct service there. In 1919 the Union-Castle Co acquired control of Bullard King & Co Ltd. That company later became part of the Springbok Line, which in 1961 was sold to the South African Marine Corporation Ltd in exchange for shares in that company. The Union-Castle Line also acquired the King Line in 1948.

When founded in 1878, the Clan Line Steamers Ltd appointed Cayzer, Irvine & Co Ltd as its managers. The first sailings were to India, but realising the possibilities of sailings to South Africa from the north of England, they inaugurated in 1881 a service from the Clyde and the Mersey to Cape Colony. Soon Clan Line were very firmly established in the South African trade as well as the Indian. In 1918 the line acquired control of the Scottish Shire Line and later in the same year of the Houston Line. Australia was now included in their services. Today regular services are operated to Australia, Ceylon, India, Pakistan and South and East Africa.

In 1950 the Clan Line entered the tanker business when they established the Scottish Tanker Company as a subsidiary. After the formation of the British & Commonwealth Shipping Co Ltd, the Neptune Shipping Co Ltd was formed in 1957, and in 1961 a controlling interest was acquired in Hector Whaling Ltd. In addition to their shipping interests, British

& Commonwealth have a 46 per cent interest in Air Holdings
Ltd, the largest independent aircraft operator in the United
Kingdom.

2 PRESENT STATUS AND ACTIVITIES

The company is engaged in shipowning and ancillary
activities: cargo liners, tramps, passenger liners, tankers and
bulk carriers. Subsidiaries concerned with shipping and
ancillary activities are established in South and East Africa.
Although the head office is in London, the company is
concerned chiefly with South and East Africa, the Indian
sub-continent and Australia. Its vessels (particularly tramps
or tankers) may call at any port in the world.

3 RECORDS

Minute books of Clan Line Steamers Ltd from
1890, and of Union-Castle from 1900
Day books etc (only kept so long as is
necessary)
Legal records: agreements and supporting
papers in respect of takeovers or mergers or
purchases of the constituent companies and
conference agreements from 1890; other
basic documents.
Letters (only kept so long as necessary unless
of special significance).
Technical drawings and blueprints: normally
retained for 5—7 years after a vessel has
entered service. The plans are retained
throughout the vessel's life, and in some
cases may be available for vessels which have
been disposed of.
Photographs: a large quantity.
Miscellaneous documents.
The records are in good condition and the Public Relations
Department of the group maintains a classified index of all

miscellaneous documents and information retained, together
with the photographs and other items of interest. Students
are advised to consult this index. Important records of the
main constituent companies are retained.

4 ACCESS

Access is granted to approved students. Records may be
removed in certain cases. Most records are kept at the
company's office but some miscellaneous records are stored
in Bishops Depository. Enquiries may be addressed to the
Secretary, Public Relations Department, Cayzer House, 2 St
Mary Axe, London EC3.

BURNS & LAIRD LINES LTD

1 HISTORY

In 1824 the produce firm of James & George Burns became
sufficiently interested in shipping to lay the foundation of the
Burns Line. Initially a successful bi-weekly service was inaugurated between Glasgow and Belfast beginning with the
Eclipse and following a year later with the *Fingal*, both
wooden paddle-steamers. In 1839, through George Burns'
energy, the Burns McIver Line was founded and from this
venture sprange the great transatlantic Cunard Line. Similarity
in house flags of Cunard and Burns & Laird is significant of
this fact. (Cunard have a lion rampant holding the world set
on a red background, whereas Burns & Laird Lines' lion is
set on a blue background.)

The activities of George Burns became so famous that he
was able to secure the mail contract in 1849 after offering
to convey mail free of all charge between Greenock and
Belfast. This agreement remained in force for thirty-three
years until payment commenced on a pound weight basis.

The ships commissioned were such splendid vessels that some were bought by the Confederates during the American Civil War to be used as blockade runners. George Burns invested these high profits in new tonnage with greater improvements.

In 1922, after the death of Lord Inverclyde, the company was merged with the Laird Line and Ayr Steamship Company and continued its operations under the title of Burns & Laird Lines Ltd.

During World Wars I and II the company's vessels gave sterling service as rescue ships, troopships and headquarters ships. With the onset of the container age Burns & Laird found it necessary to review and curtail their conventional services, and introduced in turn specialised container and unit load ships.

2 PRESENT STATUS AND ACTIVITIES

The company, a subsidiary of Coast Lines Ltd is a firm of shipowners. Together with their associated company, Northern Ireland Trailers (Scotland) Ltd, they operate daily unit load sailings from Ardrossan to Larne, while a new drive-through car ferry is employed on a daily service from Ardrossan to Belfast. A livestock vessel calls on demand at Londonderry.

3 RECORDS HELD

Minute books of G & J Burns from 1904 to 1910 and of Burns & Laird Lines from 1922.
Registers of proceedings of G & J Burns from 1910 to 1914.
Dividend and interest book of G & J Burns from 1905 to 1927.
Day book of G & J Burns from 1921; of Burns & Laird Ltd from 1922.
Cash books of G & J Burns from 1913 to 1922.
Journals of G & J Burns from 1913 to 1922 and of Laird Line from 1908 to 1922.
Bill books of Burns & Laird Ltd from 1922

and of G & J Burns from 1908 to 1922.
Ledgers of Ayr Steam Ship Co for 1901 and
of Laird Line from 1908 to 1922.
Balance sheets from 1906 to 1922.
Wages books of G & J Burns from 1903
(locked vols).
Share ledger and related documents from 1903.
Miscellaneous: various agreements and corres-
pondence from 1893, between G & J Burns
and Laird Lines Ltd and Ardrossan Harbour
Co and Workman Clark & Co; certificates of
registry from 1860 to 1933.

Records are held for G & J Burns, Laird Lines Ltd, Ayr
Steam Shipping Co Ltd, William Sloan & Co Ltd, and Burns
& Laird Lines Ltd.

4 ACCESS

Enquiries may be addressed to Company Secretary, Burns
& Laird Lines Ltd, 52 Robertson Street, Glasgow C2.

5 REFERENCE

Duckworth, C.L.D. and Langmuir, G.E.
Clyde and Other Coastal Steamers (Brown, Sue
& Ferguson 1939).

COAST LINES LTD

1 HISTORY

Coast Lines Ltd had their beginnings early in the nineteenth century with a subsequent history of continuous
service to British commerce. The parent firm of Cramm,
Powell & Co came into being in 1830, with a modest fleet
of sailing vessels plying in home waters, later to be known
as the Powell Line.

The advent of steam vessels brought in its train many changes, consolidation of some firms of shipowners and liquidation of others. Control of the Bacon Line was assumed by the Powell interests in 1910 and of the Hough Line in 1912, resulting in a combined fleet of some 16,000 tons gross. In the years immediately preceding and following World War I, the Irish cross-channel companies, British & Irish Steam Packet Co Ltd, City of Cork Steam Packet Co Ltd, Belfast Steamship Co Ltd, and Burns & Laird Lines Ltd, came into the Coast Lines Group. These companies had their origins early in the nineteenth century, each one being itself an amalgamation of a number of small concerns. The passenger services which they have for many years provided between Liverpool-Dublin, Fishguard-Cork, Liverpool-Belfast, Glasgow-Belfast and Glasgow-Dublin are justly renowned, trading without subsidy and in a business open to sea and air competition without restriction.

The title of Coast Lines Ltd was adopted in 1917. Through the succeeding years various shipping and allied interests joined the group, notably British Channel Islands Shipping Co Ltd, Tyne-Tees Steam Shipping Co Ltd, Aberdeen Steam Navigation Co Ltd, Belfast, Mersey & Manchester Steamship Co Ltd, Queenship Navigation Ltd, Zillah Shipping Co Ltd, William Sloan & Co Ltd, and North of Scotland, Orkney & Shetland Shipping Co Ltd.

Today the Coast Lines organisation operates scheduled passenger and cargo lines, coastal tramps, holiday voyages, wharves and stevedoring. There are fifty-six vessels at present in service with the group and three ships under construction. All these ships are specially designed for their particular trades on the coasting, Irish Sea and near-Continental trades. Contact is maintained by the fleet of Coast Lines and associated companies with all the principal ports of the United Kingdom, Northern Ireland, Eire, Channel Islands, Federal Republic of Germany, the Netherlands and Belgium.

Within recent times considerable developments have taken place in catering for the carriage of approved traffic in containers (insulated and non-insulated) and unit loads. Special ships have been built and a vast amount of equipment has been provided to deal with the demand for these facilities to and from ports in the United Kingdom and Northern Ireland, Eire and the near Continent. Road delivery services owned and operated by the group form an integral part of these container and unit load services. The company's ships participated actively in both world wars and were pioneers in the development of combined sea and road activities.

The following list gives a chronology of the history of the company and its associates:

Prior to 1830	S. Wainson & Cramm
1820	Cramm Powell & Co
1880	F.H. Powell & Co
1913	Powell Bacon & Hough Lines Ltd, (inc Tamplins 1840)
1917	Name of Powell Bacon & Hough Lines Ltd changed to Coast Lines Limited
1917	Control of British & Irish Steam Packet Co Ltd
1917	" " Volona Shipping Co Ltd
1918	" " H.L. Stocks & Co Ltd
1918	" " City of Cork Steam Packet Co Ltd
1919	" " Tedcastle McCormick & Co Ltd
1919	" " City of Dublin Steam Packet Co Ltd
1919	" " Belfast Steamship Co Ltd
1919	" " Laird Line Limited
1919	" " Ayr Steam Shipping Co Ltd
1919	" " M. Langlands & Sons Ltd
1920	" " G. & J. Burns Limited
1920	" " Burns Steamship Co Ltd
1920	" " Little Western Steamship Co Ltd

1922	Control of		London Welsh Steamship Co Ltd
1923	,,	,,	Grahamston Shipping Co
1926	,,	,,	Michael Murphy Limited
1926	,,	,,	Dublin General Steam Shipping Co Ltd
1926	,,	,,	M.J. Begg & Co Ltd
1928	,,	,,	David MacBryane Limited (jointly with LMS Railway)
1928-9	,,	,,	Antrim Iron Ore Co (passenger & cargo trade)
1931	,,	,,	Clyde & Campbeltown Shipping Co Ltd
1936	,,	,,	Plymouth, Channel Islands & Brittany Steamship Co Ltd
1936	,,	,,	Henry Burden Junior & Co Ltd
1937	,,	,,	London & Channel Islands Steamship Co Ltd (later renamed British Channel Islands Shipping Co Ltd)
1943	,,	,,	A. Coker & Co Ltd
1943	,,	,,	Robert Gilchrist & Co
1944	,,	,,	Tyne-Tees Steam Shipping Co Ltd
1945	,,	,,	J.J. Mack & Sons Ltd
1945	,,	,,	Belfast Mersey & Manchester Steamship Co Ltd
1945	,,	,,	S. Lawther & Sons Ltd
1946	,,	,,	The Aberdeen Steam Navigation Co Ltd
1949	,,	,,	W.A. Savage Limited)
	,,	,,	Zillah Shipping Co Ltd)
1949	Formation of Coast Lines Africa (Pty) Ltd		
1949	Sale of		Clyde & Campbeltown Shipping Co Ltd
1958	Control of		William Sloan & Co Ltd

1958	Formation of	Link Line Limited
1959	Control of	Northern Ireland Trailers Limited
1961	,, ,,	North of Scotland, Orkney & Shetland Shipping Co Ltd
1961	Purchase of	London/Belfast trade from Clyde Shipping Co Ltd
1962	Control of	Ulster Ferry Transport Limited
1964	,, ,,	Anglo Irish Transport Limited
1965	Sale of	British & Irish Steam Packet Co Ltd (including City of Cork Steam Packet Co Ltd)

2 PRESENT STATUS AND ACTIVITIES

The company is a firm of shipowners, road transport operators (especially of liquids in bulk) and wharfingers. Trade is carried on with Continental ports and South Africa. Business is conducted in the UK, Continental ports and South Africa. Facilities for the storage of mineral and edible oils, etc have been provided within the dock estate at Liverpool.

3 RECORDS HELD

Minute books from 1913 and for associated companies as below:

Ayr Steam Shipping Co Ltd	Board & General	1900-23
M.J. Begg & Co Ltd	Board	1920-31
	General	1920-32
Belfast Steamship Co Ltd	Board	1915 -to date
	General	1852 -to date
Belfast & Liverpool Shipping Co Ltd	Board & General	1890 -to date
Belfast Liverpool & Manchester Shipping Co Ltd	Board & General	1890 -to date
Belfast & Manchester Shipping Co Ltd	Board & General	1893 -to date

British Channel Islands Shipping Co Ltd	Board & General	1936 -to date
British & Irish Steam Packet Co Ltd (old company)	Board	1914-36
	General	1913-36
British & Irish Travel Agency Ltd	Board & General	1926-53
Burns & Laird Lines Ltd	Board	1922 -to date
	General	1923 -to date
G. & J. Burns Ltd	Board & General	1910-22
The Burns Steamship Co Ltd	Board & General	1908-33
Laird Line Ltd (Formerly Glasgow, Dublin & Londonderry Shipping Co Ltd)	Board & General	1899- 1922
City of Cork Steam Packet Co Ltd (old company)	Board & General	1918-36
Robert Gilchrist & Co Ltd	Board & General	1943-56
M. Langlands & Sons Ltd	Board & General	1920 -to date
Michael Murphy Ltd (old company)	Board	1905-36
	General	1906-36
Queenship Navigation Ltd	Board & General	1947 -to date
Tedcastle McCormick & Co Ltd	General	1897- 1929
Travellers Ltd	Board & General	1929-53
Victoria Wharves Ltd	Board & General	1914-20

Legal records: collection of deeds
Miscellaneous: sailing bills, rate books, press cuttings and other documents.

Records are stored in part at the company's Liverpool office and in part at 35 Crutched Friars, London EC3.

4 ACCESS

Enquiries may be addressed to the Company Secretary,

Coast Lines Ltd, Reliance House, Water Street, Liverpool.

5 REFERENCE
Duckworth and Langmuir *op cit*

WILLIAM CORY & SON LTD

1 HISTORY

The actual date of the first establishment of the firm in the coal business is unknown, but it was certainly before 1785, for by then it was a flourishing concern. The first William Cory definitely associated with the firm was living near Lambeth Wharf in 1811. His partner was John West, whose family was prominent in the coal business, the partnership being known as West & Cory, Coal and Coke Merchants. When this partnership dissolved, Cory took into the business Thomas and Benjamin Hawes. The company was then known as Wm Cory & Company.

By 1818 an association had been formed with Fenwicks, a firm of north-east coast shipowners. In 1822 Russell Scott bought out his uncles' share and the partnership of Cory & Scott was formed. In 1838 Russell Scott retired from the partnership and soon afterwards both Cory's sons became partners.

In the 1850s the firm had its first direct connection with ships as distinct from barges and lighters. At this time Cory's chartered many more ships than they owned. Their charters were popular because they always tried to get the cargo out as quickly as possible, and they had the facilities to beat anybody else on the river.

In 1896 Cory's amalgamated with seven other companies connected with coal, and the distinctive colour scheme was chosen for all the ships concerned. The combined fleet was insufficient for the trade, and ships of other companies were constantly taken on time charter. Steam Colliers Ltd, a new firm, built a number of speedy colliers which, under agreement, were chartered by Cory's for a period of years.

By the outbreak of war in 1914 the company had twenty-seven colliers. Despite the priority given to warship building in the war years, Cory's managed to obtain new tonnage. In World War II, out of regard for the importance of coal as a material of war, the company was allowed to build several ships. During the war Cory's were called upon to manage for the Ministry of War Transport a number of foreign ships.

2 PRESENT STATUS AND ACTIVITIES

The company is one of the best-known bunkering firms in the world, with depots all over the globe for coal and/or oil fuel. It is the general bunker agent to the Anglo-Iranian Oil Co Ltd. It also engages in shipbuilding, ships' agency work, lighterage, towage and salvage, wharfing, sand and ballast, warehousing, cold storage, road haulage, shipping and forwarding, air freight, export packing, and travel. Trade is carried on in Eire, France, USA, South and South-West Africa, Rhodesia and Portuguese East Africa.

3 RECORDS HELD

Minute books from 1896
Journals from 1956
Cash books from 1954
Ledgers from 1916
Trading and profit and loss accounts from 1897
Legal records: documents on firm's constitution from 1897 and various other documents
Miscellaneous: stemming list from 1875
Records are held for the following companies: Cory Colliers

Ltd, Cory Maritime Ltd, Bulk Oil Steamship Ltd, South Coast Shipping Co Ltd.

4 ACCESS

Enquiries may be addressed to the Company Secretary, Wm Cory & Son Ltd, Cory Buildings, Fenchurch St, London EC3.

CUNARD STEAMSHIP COMPANY LTD

1 HISTORY

In 1838 the British government, impressed with the evident superiority of steamships over sailing vessels, invited tenders for the conveyance of mail by steam vessels. Samuel Cunard, a prominent merchant and shipowner of Halifax, Nova Scotia, whose Dutch Quaker ancestors came to America in 1683, had long advocated a steam-packet service on the North Atlantic. In 1839 he obtained a government contract and subsidy. With the assistance of Robert Napier the Clyde shipbuilder, of George Burns a shipowner already engaged in the coasting trade, and of David MacIver, Burns' partner, he founded the British & North American Royal Mail Steam-Packet Co, with a capital of £270,000, of which Cunard found £55,000. Since 1840 the company has continuously and regularly carried passengers and mail on the North Atlantic. The first four ships were the *Britannia, Acadia, Caledonia* and *Columbia* — all wooden paddle-wheel vessels, for which the government subsidy amounted to £80,000 per annum.

In 1847 the government decided to double the Atlantic mail service. A new contract was entered into providing that a vessel should leave Liverpool every Saturday for New York or Boston alternately. The subsidy was raised to £173,340 per annum, at which figure it remained until the end of 1867. In 1852 the Cunard Co introduced the screw propeller in ships of the auxiliary service in the Mediterranean, which commenced in the same year. In 1862 the company definitely pledged itself to iron screw steamers. After 1881 these gave place to steel ships.

In 1867, when the Postmaster General entered into a new contract, it was stipulated that a steamer should be despatched every Saturday from Liverpool to New York, calling at Queenstown for the mails. The subsidy was reduced to £80,000, curtailed to £70,000 per annum in 1868. When the contract was renewed in 1875 the owners were remunerated according to the weight of the correspondence carried.

The twin-screw liners *Campania* and *Lucania,* launched in 1893, were the first Cunard ships to carry no sails. The steam turbine made its appearance in the *Carmania* in 1904.

In 1878 the Mediterranean and Atlantic fleets were amalgamated under the name of the Cunard Steamship Co Ltd, with a capital of £2 million, of which £1,200,000 was issued and taken by the families of the three founders as part payment for the undertaking transferred by them to the company. No shares were offered to the public until 1880. William Cunard, a younger son of the founder, died in 1906. His son Ernest took his place on the board of directors and was the last member of the family to participate in the management of the company. He retired in 1922.

The vessels of the company have played a conspicuous part in British naval history, as transports and armed cruisers, and subsequently as hospital ships and sea-plane ships. At the outbreak of the Crimean War six steamers were placed at the disposal of the government. In 1914 the Cunard fleet consisted of twenty-six sea-going steamers, of which thirteen were lost by enemy action.

After World War I, it was decided that three former transatlantic liners, *Aquitania, Berengaria* and *Mauretania,* needed replacement. Two splendid large ships, the *Queen Mary* and the *Queen Elizabeth,* were built with the financial support of the government. The *Queen Mary* made her maiden voyage in 1936; the *Queen Elizabeth* was not completed until after the outbreak of World War II and went into service as a troopship in 1940, having been converted for the purpose. After the end of the war they resumed their normal civilian service. In the late 1960s both ships were sold to private American companies.

In 1960 it was agreed that the successor to the *Queen Mary* would be owned by the Cunard White Star Co Ltd, of which the entire share capital was to be owned by Cunard. The contract was signed in 1964 and the *Queen Elizabeth II*, estimated to have cost about £29 to £30 million, was launched by HM the Queen in 1967. In 1965 the company owned twenty ships with a gross tonnage of 377,000 BRT. In 1962 BOAC-Cunard Ltd was founded, but in 1967 Cunard severed its connection with BOAC. The company acquired the following subsidiaries: the Port-Line Co Ltd (formerly the Commonwealth and Dominion Line Ltd) in 1916; Thos & Jno Brocklebank Ltd in 1940; Oceanic Steam Navigation Co Ltd (White Star Line) in 1949; and Moss Tankers.

2 PRESENT STATUS AND ACTIVITIES

The company's headquarters are in Southampton. The company carries passengers and mail across the Atlantic to North American ports. In addition to the subsidiary companies mentioned above, the parent company owns three property companies (Cunard House Ltd, Cunard Properties Ltd, Cunard Properties Canada Ltd), an insurance company (Cunard Insurance Ltd), a stevedoring company (Cunard Stevedoring Ltd), a company of ship repairers (Chas Howson & Co Ltd), and a firm of shipping agents (Funch Edye & Co Inc).

3 RECORDS HELD

Minute books of directors' meetings, annual general meetings, etc, from 1878

CUNARD STEAMSHIP COMPANY LTD

Cash books from 1949
Ledgers from 1878
Journal transfers for 1878
Voyage abstract for 1878
Stock or inventory books from 1934
Wage sheets (crew) for the last seven years
Annual accounts from 1914
Legal records: copies of articles of association
from 1878; numerous agency agreements; ship-
building contracts etc; numerous apprentice-
ship indentures; numerous property leases
from 1914
Letters from 1878; directors' letters in letter
books to 1939
Technical drawings and blueprints (numerous)
Photographs
Annual reports; trade circulars.

The records, held in London and Liverpool, are in good
condition and are indexed. Records of Port-Line Ltd, Thos &
Jno Brocklebank Ltd, Oceanic Steam Navigation Co Ltd and
Moss Tankers are held by these subsidiaries. Apprenticeship
indentures are kept by the Technical Department; technical
drawings are held by the Naval Architect; photographs by
the Public Relations Department. Further records are in pro-
cess of being sorted: enquiries should be addressed to the
National Register of Archives.

4 ACCESS

No access is granted at present. Enquiries may be addressed
to the Group Secretary, the Cunard Steam-Ship Co Ltd, 15
Lower Regent Street, London SW1.

5 REFERENCES

Bonsor, N.R.P. *North Atlantic Seaway*
(T. Stephenson 1937; 2nd ed 1967)

A History of the Cunard Line from 1840-1902
(Liverpool 1902)
A Short History of the Cunard Steamship Company (Glasgow 1893)

ELDER DEMPSTER LINES LTD

1 HISTORY

The history of this company, Britain's greatest shipping line in the West Africa—UK trade, goes back to 1852, when Macgregor Laird formed the African Steam Shipping Co. With the backing of a Liverpool merchant, Thomas Stirling, Laird and Richard Lander, an African explorer, formed an expedition with the object of opening up the Niger trade. The expedition sailed in 1832. Although it was a failure commercially, it proved that the Niger was navigable by steamers and that a large internal trade was possible.

For a time Macgregor Laird turned his back on West Africa, and in 1837 formed a company to operate steamers between Liverpool and New York. In 1844 he moved to Birkenhead and for the next four years was actively engaged in developing the shipbuilding and engineering works of Laird Brothers (now Messrs Cammell Laird & Co Ltd). However, in 1848 Laird moved to London and devoted the rest of his life to the development of trade with West Africa.

Laird entered into a contract with the government to maintain a regular monthly service to West African ports. The African Steam Ship Co was incorporated by Royal Charter in 1852. By the 1870s the company's trade from London was not proving very profitable and the firm transferred its home port to Liverpool, which became the permanent home port in 1875.

In 1868 John Dempster became Liverpool agent for a new company trading in West Africa. For a partner he chose

Alexander Elder, and so the firm of Elder Dempster & Co was born, to be the Liverpool representatives of the new Glasgow shipping company called the British & African Steam Navigation Co. The company's vessels were constructed in the Fairfield (Glasgow) yard of John Elder, brother of Alexander.

The two companies, both with headquarters in Liverpool, prospered and came to an arrangement whereby sailings were divided between them. In 1875 Alfred Lewis Jones (later Sir Alfred Jones) set up a shipping and insurance broking office in Liverpool under the name Alfred L. Jones & Co, and with some small chartered sailing vessels began trading with West Africa. By 1879 Jones, whose competition was feared, was made a junior partner in Elder Dempster & Co and, by 1884, was left as the controlling partner of Elder Dempster & Co. He started to buy shares in the friendly rival firm, the African Steam Ship Co which he soon came to control. In 1890 Elder Dempster & Co officially took over the management of the latter company.

It was in 1884 that Alfred Jones introduced the banana to the ordinary English citizen and the banana trade came to form the focus of the company's business. But the company also broadened its interests in other directions by taking over the Dominion Lines' Bristol to Canada trades, and in 1898 also the Canadian Beaver Line (Canada Shipping Co Ltd), which ran services between Canada and Liverpool.

In 1898 the Elder Dempster Shipping Co Ltd was formed and trade was opened up between England and the Gulf of Mexico. In 1900 the company purchased the British & African Steam Navigation Co, which Elder Dempster had managed since its inception in 1868. In 1903, with the gold mining boom in West Africa, the company inaugurated their 'express service' to the Gold Coast. On Sir Alfred Jones' death in 1909, the concern was converted into a limited liability company. Elder Dempster Lines Ltd was incorporated in 1932 after the Kylsant debacle. In 1936 the Ocean Steam Ship Co was appointed manager of Elder Dempster Lines Ltd.

2 PRESENT STATUS AND ACTIVITIES

The company is a wholly owned subsidiary of the Ocean Steamship Co Ltd, trading with West African and North American ports.

3 RECORDS HELD

Minute books from 1932

Ledgers: private from 1932, others from 1950

Balance sheets of P & LA Co from 1932

Wages books and portage bills from 1950

Prices current: ships' cost accounts from 1932

Legal records: formal records on firm's constitution from 1932; agency agreements from 1945; other contracts from 1943; specifications for ships from 1932.

4 ACCESS

Access is permitted on a limited scale, but records may not be removed. Enquiries should be addressed to the Company Secretary, Elder Dempster Lines Ltd, India Buildings, Liverpool 2.

FURNESS, WITHY & COMPANY LTD

1 HISTORY

The company was founded in 1891. At various dates it took over the following companies: Trustee, Debenture, Assets Purchase & Mortgage Guarantee Co Ltd; British Maritime Trust Ltd; Royal Mail Steam Packet; and Royal Mail Lines.

2 PRESENT STATUS AND ACTIVITIES

The company is one of the largest groups of shipowners,

which conducts business in the United States, Canada and
Trinidad. Its subsidiary companies, the Royal Mail Steam
Packet and Royal Mail Lines, are also shipowners and conduct
business in South America, Central America and the United
States. The other two subsidiaries are engaged in ship mortgage
business and investment trust business.

3 RECORDS HELD

Minute books of Royal Mail Steam Packet
from 1839 to 1936, of Royal Mail Lines from
1932, of Furness, Withy & Co from 1891,
and of British Maritime Trust from 1888.
Records are also held for the Trustee, Debenture, Assets
Purchase and Mortgage Guarantee Co Ltd.

4 ACCESS

Enquiries may be addressed to the Company Secretary,
Furness, Withy & Co Ltd, Furness House, Leadenhall
Street, London EC3.

5 REFERENCE

Bushell, S.C. *Royal Mail, 1839-1939* (Trade
and Travel 1939)

GLEN LINE LTD

1 HISTORY

Following the opening of the Suez Canal in 1869, James
McGregor — a partner in the firm of Allan C. Gow & Co, sailing ship owners — decided to back his faith in steamships in
the China trade by ordering the *Glengyle,* of 1,614 tons gross,
at a cost of £25,700. The *Glengyle* completed a highly
successful maiden voyage in 1871 and was the first of eleven
steamers built for the Glen Line by McGregor, Gow & Co —

as the partnership came to be called — during the next ten years. The contribution of these early steamers to the development of British trade with the Far East can be judged by the fact that though famous clippers like the *Cutty Sark* might make a passage of 100 days from Foochow to London, the new steamers, routed through the Suez Canal, regularly made passages of 50 days. The *Glenogle,* built in 1881, was a tremendous advance on her predecessors, being 3,749 tons gross, designed for a service speed of 15 knots, and costing over £90,000. On one occasion she made the passage from Foochow to London in just under thirty days.

The first Glen steamers were built primarily for the China tea trade. Towards the end of the century increased competition in the China trade and the development of tea-growing in India and Ceylon caused a heavy fall in freights. Nevertheless, in 1895 the company was maintaining fortnightly sailings from London to the Far East and making average passages to Hong Kong in forty days, while with the delivery in 1897 of the *Glenlochy* and the *Glenturret* of 4,700 tons deadweight, the company acquired the first of a new and successful class of ships.

The association between the Glen and Shire Lines dates from 1911. The Shire Line had held an honourable place in the China trade for many years, having been founded by Captain D.J. Jenkins with a small fleet of sailing ships in the sixties, to which in the seventies were added four steamers. In the early part of the present century the Shire Line, having passed through a difficult period, had twice changed ownership and was short of tonnage. The Glen Line also changed hands in 1910. In view of the similarity of their trades and the interest of Sir Owen Philipps in both companies, the Glen and Shire joint service was inaugurated, and this has been maintained ever since.

In spite of the restrictions inevitable in wartime, the company continued to study the technical development of hull machinery design. In particular, the Glen Line undertook large-scale experiments with diesel engines, and in 1916 the *Glengyle* was one of the first British motor ships to sail for the Far East. In the early twenties the Glen Line built five large twinscrew motor ships of 11,500 tons deadweight and nearly 17,000 tons bale capacity. These fine ships, known as the *Glenapp* class, had magnificent cargo gear. They had a long and honourable career, but the very high capital cost of this class and of a number of government standard ships acquired between 1918 and 1921 placed a considerable strain on the finances of the company. No further orders for new tonnage were placed until 1936, following the acquisition of the lines by the Ocean Steam Ship Co (Blue Funnel Line) Ltd. Eight ships were then ordered, designated the *Glenearn* class, with a service speed of 18 knots.

The refitting of the fleets for the Far Eastern trade after World War II proved a formidable task which was not completed till the latter part of 1948. The company was then again in a position to operate regular twice-monthly services, entirely with fast ships, between the UK and the Continent and the Far East.

Two new classes of powerful and highly-automated 21-knot cargo liners, each of four ships, were brought into service in the 1960s as replacements for the *Glenearn* class: the *Glenlyon* class in 1962, and the *Glenalmond* class in 1966-7.

2 PRESENT STATUS AND ACTIVITIES

The company is one of shipowners operating in the Far East: Singapore, Malaysia, Thailand, Hongkong, Chinese People's Republic, Japan, Philippines, Ceylon.

3 RECORDS HELD

Minute books, various
Legal records, various, and other papers dealing with the origins and development of the company.

4 ACCESS

Enquiries should be addressed to the Company Secretary, Glen Line Ltd, 16 St Helen's Place, London EC3.

HENDERSON LINE LTD

1 HISTORY

The company was founded on 24 May 1963 as P. Henderson & Co Ltd. The name was changed to Henderson Line Ltd on 17 July 1964 when the share capital was acquired by Liner Holdings Co Ltd.

2 PRESENT STATUS AND ACTIVITIES

The company owns ships operating mainly from the UK to Burma, via Suez (but temporarily via the Cape). It has no place of business abroad, but has offices in Glasgow; the owning company is based on Liverpool.

3 RECORDS HELD

Minute books (complete)
Day books from 1966
Cash books from 1966
Ledgers from 1963
Legal records: all of importance
Rates agreements
Photographs, technical drawings, trade
circulars and other miscellaneous documents.

The records are in good condition but unclassified. Technical drawings are with Elder Dempster Lines Ltd, Liverpool, who also arrange for stores and officers.

4 ACCESS

Access is granted to approved students, but records may not be removed. Enquiries may be addressed to the Company Secretary, Roxburgh, Henderson & Co Ltd, 80 Buchanan Street, Glasgow C1.

5 REFERENCE
Laird, D. *Paddy Henderson* (Glasgow 1961).

HOGARTH SHIPPING COMPANY LTD

1 HISTORY

In 1862 James Goodwin and Hugh Hogarth commenced business in Ardrossan as ship stores merchants and subsequently shipowners, trading under the name of Goodwin & Hogarth. In 1878 the partners separated, each continuing to trade under his own name. By 1900 James Goodwin was out of business. In the early 1880s Hugh Hogarth transferred his office to Glasgow. In 1898 he consolidated the ownership of his ships by the formation of Hogarth Shipping Co Ltd, of which company he was appointed manager. In 1901, on assuming as partners two of his sons, he altered the name of his firm from Hugh Hogarth to H. Hogarth & Sons. In 1903 a further owning company, Kelvin Shipping Co Ltd, was formed, H. Hogarth & Sons being appointed managers.

In 1919 H. Hogarth & Sons opened an office in London, mainly for shipbroking purposes, under the name of Hogarth Sons & Co Ltd. In 1924 a further owning company, Iberia Shipping Co Ltd, was formed, H. Hogarth & Sons being appointed managers. In 1952 the name of Iberia Shipping Co Ltd was altered to H. Hogarth & Sons Ltd, the management of Hogarth Shipping Co Ltd, Kelvin Shipping Co Ltd and Hogarth Sons & Co Ltd being transferred from H. Hogarth & Sons to H. Hogarth & Sons Ltd. H. Hogarth & Sons thereby ceased to exist. In 1965 the ships of Kelvin Shipping Co Ltd were sold to Hogarth Shipping Co Ltd and Kelvin Shipping Co Ltd was placed in members' voluntary liquidation.

2 PRESENT STATUS AND ACTIVITIES

The company is one of shipowners and shipbrokers

operating on a world-wide scale. Business is conducted from Ardrossan, Glasgow and London.

In 1966 H. Hogarth & Sons Ltd and Hogarth Sons & Co Ltd became wholly owned subsidiaries of Hogarth Shipping Co Ltd and the fleet was transferred from Hogarth Shipping Co Ltd to H. Hogarth & Sons Ltd. Thus the present enterprise consists of the parent company, Hogarth Shipping Co Ltd, and two wholly owned subsidiaries: H. Hogarth & Sons Ltd, the owning company, and Hogarth Sons & Co Ltd, the ship-broking company.

3 RECORDS HELD

Minute books from 1898 to 1966
Legal records: partnership agreements from
1901; deeds of settlement from 1898

Records held for Goodwin & Hogarth, Hugh Hogarth, H. Hogarth & Sons, Kelvin Shipping Co Ltd, Iberia Shipping Co Ltd, Hogarth Sons & Co Ltd, H. Hogarth & Sons Ltd.

4 ACCESS

Enquiries may be addressed to the Company Secretary, Hogarth Shipping Co Ltd, 120 St Vincent Street, Glasgow C2.

HOULDER BROS & COMPANY LTD

1 HISTORY

The firm was founded in 1849 by Edwin Savory Houlder when he commenced trading on his own from the office of his employers, Messrs Ioinides Sgouta & Co. By 1853 he had established his own office in Gracechurch Street, London, as a ship and insurance broker. The firm was soundly established by the following year when Mr Houlder was elected an annual subscriber at Lloyds. As the Australia trade developed the firm consolidated its business in that field and also extended its activities by venturing into shipowning. Regular sailings under the firm's management were giving greater work to the passenger side of the business and Mr Philips, the firm's passenger manager, moved to Plymouth where he set up an office to deal with the increasing number of emigrants travelling from there. By 1863 the outward sailings had developed into a regular clipper packet service which was being operated to New Zealand as well as Australia. By 1865 the firm was advertising itself under the title of the Australia and New Zealand Packet Service.

Houlders, in conjunction with J.T. Arundel & Co, a firm in which they held a quarter share, leased from the government a number of Pacific islands which yielded guano, coconuts and phosphate. This solved for the company the problem of inward cargoes. During the later 1860s the firm became interested in the carriage of contract cargo and undertook large contracts with the Indian and South African governments for the supply of coal. By the mid-seventies the vessels were making regular calls at South African ports. By 1881 the firm had taken an interest in the South American trade, carrying meat, especially from the River Plate — a trade in which the company still plays an important part today. In 1870 the firm acquired its first steam tonnage. With the introduction of steamers into the fleet the firm adopted what was becoming the recognised practice of the day: floating a separate limited company for each ship.

In 1898 Houlders Brothers & Co Ltd was formed as a limited liability company to take over the partnership of Houlder Brothers & Co, and in 1899 the various single-ship companies were merged into the Houlder Line Ltd with ten vessels. In 1902 Houlder Brothers, in conjunction with the Federal Steam Navigation Co, commenced a service between New Zealand, Australia and South Africa, 'The New Zealand and South African Line'. In 1904 the company and the Federal Steam Navigation Co co-joined in the 'American and Australian Line', which was an enterprise additional to the joint services of the company and the Federal Line. In 1906 the 'Federal Houlder Shire Line' under this title commenced a regular service between the UK, South Africa, Australia and New Zealand without amalgamation. In 1912 the company acquired the cartage business of J.A. Webster of Liverpool; in 1913 a number of important meat contracts were signed and the general cargo freight side was expanding.

Early in 1914 the British Empire Steam Navigation Co Ltd, and in 1915 the Furness-Houlder Argentine Line Ltd, were formed to provide tonnage for an additional contract. In 1920 the capital of Houlder Brothers & Co Ltd was increased. In the same year the company purchased the business of H.L. Wright & Co of Santos and formed branches of the company which in 1931 became Houlder Brothers & Co (Brazil) Ltd.

2 PRESENT STATUS AND ACTIVITIES

The company is one of shipowners, shipbrokers, general forwarding and air freight agents and passenger agents; it also operates inclusive tours. Business is conducted from the UK with the Argentine and Uruguay.

3 RECORDS HELD

Minute books (Houlder Bros & Co Ltd) from 1898 (6 vols)
Ledgers (private) from 1898
Accounts (signed) from 1898 to 1966
Directors' reports from 1898 to 1966
Salary books (staff) from 1900
Legal records: various, from 1898

4 ACCESS

Enquiries may be addressed to the Company Secretary, Houlder Bros & Co Ltd, 53 Leadenhall Street, London EC3.

5 REFERENCE

Stevens, Edward F. *A Hundred Years of Houlders* (Houlder Line 1950)

1 HISTORY

The company was established in 1850 by W. Inman as the Liverpool, New York & Philadelphia Steamship Co. In 1875 the company was re-established under the title of Inman Steamship Co Ltd. In 1886 it was taken over by the International Navigation Co and assumed the title of Inman & International Steamship Co Ltd. In 1893 it became known as the American Line. The last of its services was taken over by the White Star Line in 1923.

2 PRESENT STATUS AND ACTIVITIES

Business defunct.

3 RECORDS HELD

Report of chairman and directors, 1875
Dividends lists, 1860-74
List of shareholders of Inman Steamship Co
Logs (abstracts) for vessels: *City of Brussels,* March 1870; *City of Berlin,* Sept/Oct 1875; *City of Chester,* August 1878; *City of Chicago,* October 1885
Details of fleet, 1860 and 1882
Passages of New York and Liverpool Packets in 1818-21
Passages by Inman Mail steamers, Queenstown-New York, 1873-83
Passages by White Star Line, 1872-1883
Illustrations of steamers

4 ACCESS

The records are held in the Liverpool Record Office, Ref No 387 INM. Enquiries should be addressed to the City Librarian, Liverpool Record Office, William Brown Street, Liverpool 3.

5 REFERENCE

Bonsor, N.R.P. *North Atlantic Seaway*
(T. Stephenson 1937; 2nd edn 1967)

LONDON AND EDINBURGH SHIPPING CO LTD

1 HISTORY

The company was founded in 1809 to run sailing smacks between Leith and London. In 1858 it purchased its first steamers and a passenger and cargo service was operated until 1939. After World War II, a cargo service was provided in conjunction with London Scottish Lines, until 1958.

2 PRESENT STATUS AND ACTIVITIES

Business defunct.

3 RECORDS HELD

Minute book from 1809
Ledger, March 1797
Cash book, March 1797
Memorandum and articles of association,
20 Oct 1908

Insurance record of vessels, 1878
Letter to shareholders, 11 July 1809
Newspaper cuttings, advertisements etc from
1792

4 ACCESS

The first group of records listed above was kept at London & Edinburgh Shipping Co Ltd, 17 Bernard Street, Leith, Edinburgh 6, and the second group at Windsor House, 1270 London Road, Norbury, London SW16. Enquiries may be made to the Secretary, National Register of Archives (Scotland

PO Box 36, HM General Register House, Edinburgh 2 (Ref
No NRA (Scot) 0320).

MANCHESTER LINERS LTD

1 HISTORY

Manchester Liners Ltd was founded in 1898 by Sir
Christopher Furness and others to provide a regular service
from the then new Manchester Ship Canal to Canada and the
USA, a service which has been maintained without interrup-
tion since that date. A service to South America was operated
for a short time, but the company now sails to ports on the
East Coast of USA, and Canada, and since 1952, to the Great
Lakes. A container service with specially designed ships has
recently been inaugurated.

2 PRESENT STATUS AND ACTIVITIES

The company is one of shipowners which operates between
the UK and North America; the headquarters are in Manchester.

3 RECORDS HELD

Minute books from 1898
Important correspondence from 1898

4 ACCESS

Enquiries should be addressed to the Company Secretary,
Manchester Liners Ltd, St Ann's Square, Manchester 2.

5 REFERENCE

Manchester Liners Ltd. *Fifty Years in the
Western Ocean* (1948), *Sixty Years in the
Western Ocean* (1958)

MOOR LINE LTD and
WALTER RUNCIMAN & CO LTD

1 HISTORY

Captain Walter Runciman was born at Dunbar in 1848 and obtained his first command, the clipper barque *F.E. Althausse*, at the age of 23; he came ashore in 1884 and next year purchased his first vessel, the SS *Dudley*, a single-decked three-masted screw schooner. A number of other vessels were acquired on a similar basis, including the first new building, the SS *Blakemoor*. Constructed by John Readhead & Sons, South Shields, this vessel was launched in February 1889. It was named after the Blakemoor estate in Northumberland, which belonged to relatives of Captain Runciman's wife.

The South Shields Steam Shipping Co Ltd was formed on 25 June 1889 with a registered capital of £150,000. John Elliott was the first chairman and Captain Walter Runciman managing director and secretary. A fleet of tramp ships was quickly built up and in 1891 the capital of the company was doubled. Next year the offices were moved from South Shields to 86 Pilgrim Street, Newcastle-upon-Tyne, where they remained until 1904 when they were transferred to Moor Buildings, 56 Pilgrim Street. On 28 April 1897 the South Shields Steam Shipping Co Ltd changed its name to Moor Line Ltd. Captain Walter Runciman and his son Walter Runciman, who carried on business under the name of Walter Runciman & Co Ltd, were appointed managing directors. In the following year, on the death of John Elliott, Captain Walter Runciman became chairman, a position which he occupied until his death in 1937.

On 29 September 1902 Moor Line incorporated the Novocastrian Shipping Co and in 1905 North Moor Steam-ships. After heavy losses in the war the ships were sold to Western Counties Shipping Co. On 2 September 1920 the company went into voluntary liquidation.

On 10 November 1920 the present Moor Line was formed as a public company quoted on the Newcastle Stock Exchange.

Like its predecessor it built up in a short time a large fleet of
tramp ships for world-wide trading. After weathering success-
fully the economic blizzard of the 1930s it suffered severe
losses in World War II. A steady programme of replacement
followed and in 1964 the first big bulk carrier was ordered.

In July 1965 the company purchased the Anchor Line
from the United Molasses Ltd, believing that the association
of the two companies offered a broader and surer foundation
on which to build future expansion in shipping than was to be
found in a tramp business alone. In 1965 the company joined
in a consortium with Sheaf Steam Shipping Co Ltd and
Reardon Smith Line Ltd.

Since 1920 the Moor Line in Newcastle had continued
to be managed by Walter Runciman & Co Ltd, which had
also been responsible for the management of the Anchor
Line in Glasgow since 1935. In 1966 Moor Line purchased the
managing company and in 1967 severed its connection with
Newcastle, moving the registered office to London and
concentrating the main management of the two fleets in
Glasgow.

2 PRESENT STATUS AND ACTIVITIES

The company owns tramp ships and is engaged in world-
wide trading. It has offices in London and Glasgow.

3 RECORDS HELD

Minutes and minute books of South Shields
Steamship Co Ltd 1892-1936; of South
Shields Shipping Co and Moor Line Ltd (1
vol) 1889-97; of Walter Runciman & Co Ltd
1916-37, 1915-42 and 1935-47; of Moor
Line Ltd 1899-1916, 1917-20 and 1920-38.
Journals (2 vols) of Walter Runciman & Co
Ltd 1892-93 and 1894-1941
Cash books of Walter Runciman & Co Ltd
1892-3, 1959-64; of Moor Line Ltd (vol no 1)

1920-4, (vol no 15) 1959-61, (vol no 16)
1961-2.

Petty cash book of Moor Line Ltd 1959-61

Ledgers: of Walter Runciman (private) 1899-
1932; of Walter Runciman & Co Ltd 1892-3

Share Allotment book and annual returns of
Moor Line Ltd 1891-1922

Register of transfers of Moor Line Ltd 1921-
47

Wages books (apprentices) (1 vol) 1925-37

Legal records: memorandum and articles of
association of South Shields Steamship Co
Ltd, 21 June 1889, with additional special
resolutions to 20 March 1899; of North Moor
Steam Ships Ltd, 27 September 1897; of
Novocastrian Shipping Co Ltd, 29 September
1902, with special resolutions passed 27
February 1913, 24 March 1913 and 24
January 1916 to original memorandum and
articles of 29 September 1902; of Tyne Life-
boat Society, registered 23 February 1905; of
International Stores Ltd, 1 May 1912; of
Walter Runciman & Co Ltd, 10 December
1915 (3 copies), 8 January 1942 (2 copies);
of Moor Line Ltd, 10 November 1920 (2
copies); of Cowpen Drydocks and Shipbuilding
Co Ltd, registered 20 November 1926; proposed
alterations of articles of association to include
air trading, 1945; certificates of incorporation
of Walter Runciman & Co Ltd, 1915 and 1942;
certificate of change of name from Runciman
Shipping Co Ltd to Walter Runciman & Co
Ltd, 31 March 1947; documents of Moor
Line Ltd relating to sale of fleet of Western
Counties Shipping Co, 1920; Runciman

Shipping Co Ltd Pension Trust Deed, 25
February 1944; sets of agreements for new
tonnage, 1893-1912, 1920-34; plans for
agreement relating to ship 719 from W.
Doxford & Co Ltd, 2 March 1943; new
regulations of Moor Line Ltd (formerly South
Shields Steam Ship Co Ltd), name changed
28 April 1897; important agreements from
1893; miscellaneous documents from 1894
Letters and letter books: of Walter Runciman,
4 books for 1886-7, 1889-90, 1890-2, and
1888-96, and various letters 1887-9, 1926;
correspondence with W. Doxford & Sons Ltd
new building, 1934-46
Technical drawings: plan of *Thornycroft,*
1921; general arrangement plan of *Kirriemoor,*
23 November 1934; general arrangement of
no 771; plans and quotation for 9,500-ton
ship from R.W. Hawthorn Leslie & Co Ltd,
September/October 1936 (2 copies); general
arrangement of *Fernmoor,* 3 June 1937;
general arrangement of ship no 706, by W.
Doxford & Sons Ltd, 14 July 1942;
provisional plans from W. Doxford & Sons
Ltd, c 1934, possibly 'Economy Doxford'
for *Fernmoor* and *Kirriemoor;* specifications
for various vessels, including ships 771 and
773, 20 May 1946
Photographs from 1921; of launches and
trial trips; of *Linkmoor, Jedmoor, Glenmoor,
Kirriemoor*
Miscellaneous: arrivals and sailings (3 vols)
1912-17, 1922-30, and 1922-34; newspaper
cuttings books (2 vols) 1894-1902, 1902-7;
file of circulars of Moor Line Ltd for 1920;

club insurance call book and other incunabula
The records are in good condition and listed. They are stored
at 16 Royal Exchange Square, Glasgow C2.

4 ACCESS

Access is granted to approved students and portions may
be temporarily removed. Enquiries may be addressed to the
Managing Director, 59 Waterloo Street, Glasgow C2.

NORTH OF SCOTLAND, ORKNEY & SHETLAND
SHIPPING CO LTD

1 HISTORY

The firm's history goes back to 1790, when it was founded
as the Aberdeen, Leith & Clyde Shipping Co. In 1810 it was
amalgamated with the Aberdeen, Dundee, Leith & Glasgow
Shipping Co. Up to 1821 the service was carried on entirely
by sailing vessels. In 1876 the firm was renamed the North
of Scotland, Orkney & Shetland Steam Navigation Co, the
title being amended in 1953. It took over the Shetland
Islands Steam Navigation Co, Lerwick, in 1890.

2 PRESENT STATUS AND ACTIVITIES

As a subsidiary of Coast Lines Ltd, the company operates
passenger and cargo services from Leith and Aberdeen to
Orkney and Shetland, an inter-island service based on
Lerwick, and a daily service between Stromness and Scrabster.

3 RECORDS HELD

Minute books from 1810
Purchases books from 1939
Cash books and journal from 1920
Ledgers for 1922-3, 1925-6, and from 1940

Revenue books from 1924
Stock books from 1957
Wages books (crew) from 1920
Prices current from 1963
Legal records: property conveyances and
tenancy agreements
Letters from 1961

4 ACCESS

Enquiries may be addressed to the Company Secretary, North of Scotland, Orkney & Shetland Shipping Co Ltd, Matthews' Quay, Aberdeen.

5 REFERENCE

Donaldson, G. *Northwards by Sea* (Edinburgh 1966)

OCEAN STEAM SHIP CO LTD

1 HISTORY

The company was founded in 1865.

2 PRESENT STATUS AND ACTIVITIES

The company is one of shipowners operating in the Far East and Australia. It has two wholly owned subsidiaries: Elder Dempster Lines Ltd and Blue Funnel Line Ltd.

3 RECORDS HELD

Minute books (registers of proceedings) of
Ocean Steam Ship Co Ltd from 1865, and
of China (Shippers) Mutual Steam Navigation
Co Ltd from 1883
Ledgers of A. Holt from 1853 to 1965, of
Ocean Steam Ship Co Ltd from 1865, and

of China (Shippers) Mutual Steam Navigation
Co Ltd from 1897
Ships' cost accounts from 1865
Wages books (crew) from 1859
Legal records: partnership agreements from
1865; deeds of settlement or association
from 1865; formal records on firm's
constitution from 1865; specifications for
ships; apprenticeship indentures from 1940
Ships' movements from 1866

Records are also held for Alfred Holt 1853-66 and for China
(Shippers) Mutual Steam Navigation Co Ltd from 1883.

4 ACCESS
Enquiries may be addressed to the Company Secretary,
The Ocean Steam Ship Co Ltd, India Buildings, Water Street,
Liverpool 2.

5 REFERENCES
Hyde, F.E. *Blue Funnel* (Liverpool 1956)

PALM LINE LTD

1 HISTORY
The company, which had previously operated as a depart-
ment of the United Africa Co Ltd, was founded on 16
February 1949.

2 PRESENT STATUS AND ACTIVITIES
The company, a wholly owned subsidiary of Unilever Ltd,
currently operates a fleet of fifteen cargo liners and one
vegetable-oil tanker. Trade is carried on primarily between
the UK and Continent and West Africa. Certain vessels
operate on world-wide charter. Business is conducted from

London, Liverpool and Tilbury, with third-party agencies on the Continent.

3 RECORDS HELD

Minute books from 1949
Cash books retained for the last ten years only
Ledgers from 1949
Other financial records for various periods
Prices current since incorporation
Legal records since incorporation
Letters retained for the last five years
Technical drawings for all current vessels
Photographs: a collection built up since
1950, including vessels formerly operated
by the United Africa Co to 1939
Trade circulars from 1951

The records are generally in good condition and are classified.

4 ACCESS

Access is granted in principle, subject to approval by the Board of Directors. Records may not be removed. Enquiries may be addressed to the Company Secretary, Palm Line Ltd, Shelley House, Noble Street, London EC2.

PENINSULAR & ORIENTAL STEAM NAVIGATION CO LTD

1 HISTORY

The Peninsular Steam Navigation Company was formed early in the nineteenth century by two men, Brodie Willcox and Arthur Anderson, who chartered a paddle steamer to trade and carry mails between England and the Iberian Peninsula. Support for the royal houses of Spain and Portugal brought valuable trading facilities and the right to use their colours, which today form the quarterings of the present company's house flag, the blue and white of Portugal and the red and yellow of Spain.

In 1837 the company obtained a contract to carry the mails to the Peninsula and this was extended to Egypt two years later. In 1840 the name of the company was changed to the Peninsular & Oriental Steam Navigation Co and a royal charter was granted to continue and develop the existing trades. Since then they have been developed to India, Pakistan, the Far East, Australia and across the Pacific to Canada and USA.

In 1853 another new mail contract put these services to India, the Straits and China on a fortnightly basis. Meanwhile in 1852 the first regular mail run to Australia had been inaugurated by a P & O branch service from Singapore. The opening of the Suez Canal in 1869 brought difficult times for the company, which had invested large amounts in the overland route between the Mediterranean and the Far East, but with a policy of wholesale scrapping and replacement of obsolete ships the company kept ahead of its rivals on eastern trade routes.

In 1914 the first major step in the formation around P & O of a group of shipping companies was taken, when the equity of the British India Steam Navigation Co Ltd was acquired. This company was originally founded in 1856 as the Calcutta & Burma Steam Navigation Co Ltd to operate a mail service between Calcutta and Rangoon. The BI now operates a network of services throughout the East in addition to regular sailings between Europe and Ceylon, India, Pakistan, East and South Africa, Australia, as well as school cruises in specialised ships.

The New Zealand Shipping Co Ltd, which was incorporated in 1873, and the Federal Steam Navigation Co Ltd, incorporated in 1895, were amalgamated in 1912. They joined the P & O group in 1916. The fleets of these companies, which serve the trade between New Zealand, Australia, Europe and North America, are supplemented on occasion by ships of their subsidiary, the Avenue Shipping Co Ltd, incorporated in 1954.

The Hain Steamship Co Ltd and James Nourse Ltd were added to the group in 1917. Together with the Asiatic Steam Navigation Co Ltd, acquired in 1934, they now represent the main group tramping and bulk cargo interest. Following a recent re-organisation, the tramp fleets of the three companies have been combined and are now operated and managed by Hain-Nourse Ltd.

In 1917 the Union Steam Ship Co of New Zealand Ltd, a New Zealand registered company, was acquired. It is the major shipowning company in New Zealand and operates trades between New Zealand and Australia, India and North America and between Australia and Tasmania, as well as many New Zealand coastal trades.

In 1919, after World War I, a half interest was purchased in the Orient Steam Navigation Co Ltd, a company founded in 1878, owning passenger ships only in the Australian trade. This interest was made complete in 1960 when the outstanding equity was acquired and the Orient fleet was amalgamated with that of the P & O. The joint fleets operated under the name P & O – Orient Lines until October 1966, when the word 'Orient' was dropped.

In 1920 a controlling interest in the General Steam Navigation Co Ltd was acquired. This company heads a group of companies, the more important of which are Moss Hutchison Line Ltd and Turner Edwards & Co Ltd. They operate in the short sea trades and to the Mediterranean. General Steam is now engaging, through its partnership in North Sea Ferries, in the operation of roll-on/roll-off ships between Hull and Rotterdam with both freight and passenger facilities. Through Southern Ferries Ltd, similar services between the South Coast and France are now operated.

Since 1920 the group has had a controlling interest in Strick Line Ltd, a company which pioneered the direct trade between the UK/Continent and Persian and Arabian ports during the latter half of the last century. In 1946 a controlling interest was acquired in the Eastern & Australian Steamship Co Ltd, a company formed in 1873 originally to connect with the P & O mail steamers at Singapore and carry the mails on to Australia, but which now operates between Australia and the Far East.

Today the cargo liner and passenger fleets of the P & O group operate world-wide services, linking the UK and Western Europe with the Mediterranean, the Persian Gulf, India, Pakistan, Malaysia and Singapore, the China Seas, Japan, Australia, New Zealand, Hawaii and North America.

In 1955 a decision was taken to enter the tanker trade. The tankers were originally owned, managed and operated by some of the shipowning companies of the group, and Charter Shipping Co Ltd was formed in Bermuda to own certain of them. In 1962, however, Trident Tankers Ltd was established to take over the management and operation of the entire tanker fleet. The group is now the largest independent tanker owner in the UK.

In 1964 the group began building bulk carriers, vessels capable of carrying large quantities of bulk cargo such as grain, coal and ore. A trading agreement was entered into with the Anglo Norness Shipping Co Ltd for the joint operation of all bulk carriers controlled by the two groups through a jointly owned company, Associated Bulk Carriers Ltd.

P & O Offshore Services Ltd was formed in 1964 to service offshore installations drilling for oil or gas, and has six specialised craft in service or on order.

2 PRESENT STATUS AND ACTIVITIES

The company is one of shipowners operating passenger and cargo services to the Mediterranean, India, the Far East, Australia, the Pacific and North America. The shipping companies of the group are served throughout the world by a network of agency, forwarding and servicing companies, many of which it owns. In recent years the interests of the group have been extended into other fields and it is concerned in air transport, through its investment in Air Holdings and its subsidiary BUA, and in Australian road transport, through its holding in Mayne Nickless Ltd. In 1968 it owned 289 ships of 2,349,714 gross registered tons and comprises over 140 companies, large and small, all grouped around the still central business of shipowning.

Details of the companies taken over are given in the following list:

Shipowning Companies
The Peninsular & Oriental Steam Navigation Co Ltd
Asiastic Steam Navigation Co Ltd
Avenue Shipping Co Ltd
British India Steam Navigation Co Ltd
Charter Shipping Co Ltd
The Eastern & Australian Steamship Co Ltd
Federal Steam Navigation Co Ltd
The General Steam Navigation Co Ltd
The Hain Steamship Co Ltd
James Nourse Ltd
Moss Hutchison Line Ltd
The New Zealand Shipping Co Ltd
Orient Steam Navigation Co Ltd
P & O Offshore Services Ltd
Strick Line Ltd
Trident Tankers Ltd
Union Steam Ship Co of New Zealand Ltd

Shipping Companies
Anderson Green & Co Ltd Ship Brokers
Bethell Gwynn & Co Ltd, Agents and Freight Brokers
Birt & Company (Pty) Ltd Agents
Birt Potter & Hughes Ltd, Ship Brokers

Birt Potter Westray Ltd, Freight Brokers
Dowie & Marwood Ltd, Agents and Freight
Brokers
Escombe McGrath & Co Ltd, Agents and
Freight Brokers
Hain-Nourse Management Ltd
Mackinnon, Mackenzie & Co, Private Ltd,
Agents
P & O Company of Australia Pty Ltd
P & O Group Transportation Planning Ltd
P & O — Orient Management Ltd
P & O — Orient Lines Passenger Services Ltd
P & O — Orient Lines Inc, Agents
P & O — Orient Lines of Australia Pty Ltd, Agents
J. B. Westray & Co Ltd, Agents

Marine & General Engineering Companies
Conoley & Co Ltd, Civil Engineers
R & H Green & Silley Weir Ltd, Ship repairers
Silley, Cox & Co Ltd, Ship repairers, Dry dock
owners

Transport and Forwarding Companies
Anglo Overseas Transport Co Ltd
Claridge Holt & Co Ltd
Higgs (Air Agency) Ltd

The Sea Services of the P & O Group
Avenue Shipping Co Ltd is a subsidiary of the
New Zealand Shipping Company and its
associates whose ships are used in the trades of
the parent company and when not required
are available for world-wide use.

British India Steam Navigation Co Ltd operates passenger and cargo services which link the UK and Continent with East and South Africa, India, Pakistan, Persian Gulf, Burma, Malaya, Australia, New Zealand and the Far East.

Charter Shipping Co Ltd is a tanker and bulk carrier owning company registered in Bermuda.

The Eastern & Australian Steamship Co Ltd operates a cargo and passenger service between Australia, Japan and China. Northwards from Australia calls are made at Manila and Hong Kong and southwards at Hong Kong and New Guinea ports.

Federal Steam Navigation Co Ltd is owned by the New Zealand Shipping Co Ltd and operates from the West Coast of the UK and the East Coast of USA to Australia and New Zealand — via Suez and Panama.

The General Steam Navigation Co Ltd operates regular cargo services from the UK to principal Continental ports and to the Mediterranean.

Hain-Nourse Management Ltd operates the combined tramping fleets of the Asiastic Steam Navigation Co Ltd, James Nourse Ltd, and the Hain Steamship Co Ltd. The company will manage the bulk carriers presently building for the group. These ships will be employed by a separate company formed in 1964 in association with Anglo Norness.

Moss Hutchison Line Ltd operates regular cargo services from the West Coast of the UK to France, Portugal, Spain, North Africa and East Mediterranean ports.

The New Zealand and Shipping Co Ltd operates regular passenger and cargo services from the UK to New Zealand via Panama.

Peninsular and Oriental Steam Navigation Company is the group parent company.

P & O Group Transport Planning Ltd has been formed to initiate and co-ordinate studies of transportation and cargo handling systems and services.

P & O Offshore Services Ltd is building ships to service offshore oil rigs.

P & O — Orient Management Ltd is a direct subsidiary of the P & OSN Company in charge of the management of all 'P & O — Orient Lines' passenger ships, and the operation and management of cargo ships. Passenger and cargo services operate regularly between the UK, India, Far East, Australia and the Pacific.

P & O — Orient Lines Passenger Services Ltd is a direct subsidiary of the P & OSN Company in charge of the programming of all 'P & O — Orient Lines' passenger trades, and the promotion and sale of all passenger space. Passenger services operate between UK, the Far East, Australia and the Pacific, with cruises from both the UK and Australia.

Orient Steam Navigation Company Ltd is a direct subsidiary of the P & OSN Company, with no executive functions, but which owns passenger liners operating regular passenger and cargo services between the UK, Australia and the Pacific, and cruises from both the UK and Australia. The services of the Orient Line vessels are now operated under the common style of 'P & O — Orient Lines'.

Strick Line Ltd operates regular cargo and passenger services between the UK and Continental ports and the Persian Gulf, calling at Mediterranean and Red Sea ports.

Trident Tankers Ltd was formed as a wholly owned subsidiary of the P & OSN Company, to manage all the tankers hitherto managed and operated by a number of individual companies within the P & O group. Trident also owns four new tankers recently built in British yards. When the last of the new ships is delivered in mid-1965 the tanker fleet will comprise eighteen ships totalling approximately 746,000 tons deadweight.

Union Steam Ship Co of New Zealand Ltd operates passenger and cargo services from New Zealand to Australia, India, Malaysia, Pacific Islands and the West Coast of North America. There is also the famous 'Steamer Express' service between North and South Islands of New Zealand (Wellington/ Lyttleton).

3 RECORDS HELD

Board minutes and associated papers from 1840
Bill books (1 vol) from 1840 to late 1880s
Ledgers (every tenth year retained) from 1840
to 1939; from 1939 complete
Stock and share ledgers and journals from
1840 to 1951
Salary records (some) from 1840s to present
Legal records: engrossments of charters from
1840 to 1966; agency agreements from 1850s,
earlier years incomplete; shipbuilding contracts
from 1923; apprenticeship indentures (a small
collection); freehold documents of title and
leases, mostly relating to premises in Leadenhall
Street, St Mary Axe and Great St Helens,
London EC3.
Letters (random selection) from 1837
Miscellaneous: freight tariffs (certain trades
only) from 1924; passenger rates and fares from
1894
Directors' published reports and accounts
Circulars to shareholders

The records are in good condition but the Orient Steam
Navigation Co Ltd records for the pre-1939 period were destroyed by enemy action.

A museum and library is in the course of being catalogued.
It includes pictures, photographs, passage tickets, clothing
and kit lists, menu cards, newspaper cuttings, regimental
plaques, ships' bells, ship models, ship plans, presentations,
handbooks, crockery, plate, mail contracts, instructions to
commanders, crew lists, sailing lists, fleet records. The library
includes several hundred volumes relating to the company's
activities.

4 ACCESS

Enquiries should be made to the company's Public Relations

Officer. Not available for inspection are: more recent Board Minutes and associated papers and ledgers.

The company's address is: 122 Leadenhall Street, London EC3, temporarily at Beaufort House, Gravel Lane, London E1.

5 REFERENCE

Cable, Boyd, *A Hundred Year History of the P & O* (1937)

Divine, David, *These Splendid Ships* (1960)

SIR WILLIAM REARDON SMITH & SONS LTD

1 HISTORY

The company was founded in 1905 by Captain William Smith and a family connection has been retained throughout its existence; the present chairman, Alan J. Reardon Smith, is a grandson of the founder.

The company began trading with the *City of Cardiff,* a vessel of 5,700 tons. After two years of successful trading a second vessel, the *Leeds City,* was added. Despite periods of depression in the shipping industry the company has continued to expand. It took over the following companies: St Just Steamship Co Ltd, incorporated in July 1912; in July 1917 the latter amalgamated with the Great City Steamship Co Ltd and the Bradford Steamship Co Ltd; in December 1923 the St Just Steamship Co Ltd took over the Cornborough Shipping Line Ltd, and in March 1926 bought the Oakwin Steamship Co Ltd. Finally in June 1938 the Reardon Smith Line took over the Leeds Shipping Co Ltd, which is now a wholly owned subsidiary.

The fleet now comprises nine vessels, of which the oldest was built in 1956. The latest two additions to the fleet, the *Atlantic City* and *Indian City,* each of 45,800 tons, built by

Fairfields (Glasgow) Ltd, are bulk carriers fitted with cargo gear and Sulzer diesel engines with a loaded speed of 15 knots. Further expansion of the fleet is in progress.

In 1965 a consortium comprising Moor Line Ltd, Sheaf Steam Shipping Co Ltd, both of Newcastle-on-Tyne, and Reardon Smith Line Ltd was formed under the name of Maritime Bulk Carrying & Shipping Co Ltd. This consortium has the object of concluding such business as period contracts for the carriage of bulk cargo which would be beyond the capacity of each individual company.

2 PRESENT STATUS AND ACTIVITIES

The company is a firm of shipowners, shipbrokers and chartering agents which activities are world wide, trading either on a voyage or time charter basis. Although currently the company does not specialise in any particular trade, it always considers carefully any type of prospective business that may be offered. As well as acting as managers for its associates the company also acts as chartering and general agents for such overseas companies as States Marine Lines Inc and Global Bulk Transport Inc, both of New York. A close connection also exists with Irish Shipping Ltd of Dublin. The company is broker to the British Iron & Steel Corporation Ltd, London, and is associated with the leading South African shipowners, South African Marine Corporation Ltd of Cape Town, as chartering agents.

The company's head office is situated at Devonshire House, Greyfriars Road, Cardiff, and the London branch office is at Marine Engineers' Memorial Building, 18 London Street, London EC3, which is also the office of the Maritime Bulk Carrying & Shipping Co Ltd.

3 RECORDS HELD

Minute books (12 vols) from 1912

Purchases books (25 vols) from 1959

Cash books (14 vols) from 1938
Ledgers (30 vols) from 1917
Balance sheets from 1923
Ships' journals (86 vols) from 1938
Stock or inventory books (36 vols) from 1956
Wages books (299 vols) from 1954
Prices current (numerous vols) from 1965
Legal records: important agreements (14 vols)
from 1950; apprenticeship indentures (370
vols) from 1946; documents relating to title
(4 vols) from 1947
Letters (270 vols) from1959
Trade circulars (numerous vols) from 1965
Circulars (numerous vols) from 1923
A fire in 1946 destroyed a substantial amount of records.

4 ACCESS
Enquiries may be addressed to the Company Secretary, Sir
William Reardon Smith & Sons Ltd, Devonshire House, Grey-
friars Road, Cardiff.

SIR R. ROPNER COMPANY (MANAGEMENT) LTD

1 HISTORY
The firm of R. Ropner & Co was founded in 1874 with a
fleet of six ships taken over from the Appelby & Ropner
concern in which Mr Ropner had been a partner since 1866.
The company's vessels specialised in the Baltic trade and the
China Seas tea trade. Between 1876 and 1880 eleven new
vessels were added to the fleet. In 1879, foreseeing the
expansion of South Wales as a coal exporting centre, the
company opened a branch office in Cardiff, a step which
resulted in much new business as well as agency and charter
work for other firms. In 1888 the company purchased the

shipyard of M. Pearse & Co of Stockton.

Up to 1903 all the vessels managed by R. Ropner & Co were held on the 'sixty-fourths system' and there was never a lack of offers to take up 'sixty-fourths' in new ships. But the system posed great problems in book-keeping, and as a result in 1903 the Pool Shipping Co Ltd was formed to acquire and own ships which were to be managed by R. Ropner & Co. In the same year R. Ropner & Co took over the management of the Therese Heymann Steamship Co.

In 1914 the company was managing fifty-seven steamers (350,000 tons dead weight) — a fleet much depleted by the end of World War I. In 1919 the company known as the Ropner Shipping Co Ltd was registered to acquire and own ships to be managed by Sir R. Ropner & Co Ltd, so finally ending the 'sixty-fourths system' for the whole fleet. In 1925 the shipyard was closed. In its thirty-seven years under Ropner ownership it had built seventy-one ships for the company.

In December 1948 Ropner Holdings Ltd was registered as a public company to acquire the shares of the Ropner Shipping Co Ltd and the Pool Shipping Co Ltd. Both of these kept their individual status and were managed by the parent company, Sir R. Ropner & Co Ltd. In 1950 the style of the parent company was changed to Sir R. Ropner & Co (Management) Ltd. Since the war a large proportion of the fleet has been engaged on time charter work on the Australian coast. Another important development has been the inauguration of a regular liner service between the UK and the US Gulf ports and Florida, the main ports served being Mobile, New Orleans, Galveston, Houston and Brownsville, as well as Tampa and Miama in Florida.

2 PRESENT STATUS AND ACTIVITIES
The company is a shipping firm engaged in world wide trade.

3 RECORDS HELD

Minute books from 1948
Cash books from 1948
Bill books from 1948
Ledgers from 1948
Letters from 1948
Technical drawings and blueprints from 1948
Photographs from 1948
The records are in fair condition.

4 ACCESS

The memorandum and articles of association would be available for inspection, and copies of the above could be provided. Enquiries may be addressed to the Company Secretary, Ropner Holdings Ltd, 140 Coniscliffe Road, Darlington, Yorks.

ROYAL MAIL STEAM PACKET COMPANY

1 HISTORY

The Royal Mail Steam Packet Company received a Royal Charter in 1839 to provide mail services from the United Kingdom to the West Indies and the East Coast of South America. These services began in 1840, and were developed so that the company became one of the greatest British shipping companies, serving in addition to its original region, the West Coast of North America. The company also took interests in other lines whose scope ranged to Australia and the Far East. The break-up of the group in 1931-2 led to the formation of a new company, Royal Mail Lines Ltd which absorbed two other lines in the South American trade, David MacIver & Sons and the Nelson Line, and was itself within the Furness, Withy group. In recent years, the operations of Royal Mail have been closely integrated with those of Furness Lines.

2 PRESENT STATUS AND ACTIVITIES

Royal Mail Lines Ltd is now a subsidiary company in the Furness Withy Group.

3 RECORDS HELD

(i) Records held at Library of University College, London
Reports and accounts of RMSP Co Vol 1,
1842-72, Vol 2, 1873-1903
Contains prospectus etc. Mainly printed
material, but some typescript reports of annual
general meetings. Some manuscript marginalia.
Reports and accounts Vol 1, 1842-72
                              Vol 2, 1873-1903
Mainly printed, but some MS material. Includes
material on European and Australian Royal
Mail Co.
Printed accounts 1876-98 inclusive
Balance sheets, 1844-1926. (Apparently lacking
balance sheets for 1903 and 1920).
Draft accounts for 1887, 1901 and 1902.
Draft accounts 1920-1.
Printed reports of directors:
Half year & annual accounts, 1892-3, 1895,
1898, 1900
Annual accounts only for 1894, 1897, 1899
First half year accounts only for 1896, 1901,
1902
Annual reports (printed, but some interpolated
MS material), 1903-5; 1912-16; 1918-20;
1922-7; 1929-31.
Liverpool board minutes, 1 vol (1921)
Printed statement of accounts: 1st half year,
1892-5, 1897-9. Year's accounts 1892, 1894-5,
1899-1901.
Daily minutes, board of managers.

Vol 1   9 June 1843 —   1 Mar 1844
 "   2   1 Mar 1844 — 22 Oct 1844
 "   3   24 Oct 1844 — 17 Feb 1847
        (There is a loose index of matters referred to).
 "   4   18 Feb 1847 —   1 Jan 1850 (indexed)
 "   5   1 Jan 1850 —   9 Mar 1853 ("   )
 "   6   10 Mar 1853 — 22 May 1854 ("   )

Special reports to the court

Vol 1   11 Sep   1845 — 19 Aug 1852 ("   )
 "   2   23 Sep   1852 —   2 Mar 1859 ("   )
 "   3   30 Mar   1859 —   8 June 1864 ("   )

Reports of general meetings 1901—15 (Vol marked '12')

Reports of general meetings 1916—30 (Vol marked '13')

Also folders, typescript reports of general meetings for 1931, 1932 and 1934.

Memoranda books. 1 1847—8, 2 mainly 1857—63. These contain notes and memoranda about most aspects of operational affairs.

3 mainly 1900—14. Some material on staff, but summaries also of dividend payments, mail contracts, etc including data for nineteenth century, and staff appointments up to the 1930s.

MS List 'Cost and Outfit of Steamships' 1839 to 1912

Cash book 'A' 1840—2.

Day book 'A' 1841—2.

Cash book, April 1844 — June 1845.

Agency and purser's accounts ledgers, 1843—5 (covers overseas coaling stations and agencies).

Valuation book, 1875—86. (Indexed, names of vessels: shows calculations for depreciation allowances).

Fleet insurance ledger, mainly between 1920 and 1932.

Minutes of directors' committee meetings.
1907–30.

Movements book of RMSP Co vessels, 1933–39.

Minutes of the managing directors' committee,
typescript Jan – Apr 1940, mainly concerning
ship operations and movements.

Ledger (indexed) of RMSP Co investments
1900s – 1930s.

Folder, containing typescript minutes of meetings
of preference shareholders of White Star Line
as creditors of RMSP Co under its guarantee,
12 Feb 1931–16 Mar 1932, together with
printed Explanatory Memorandum regarding
the scheme of arrangement (for settling for
RMSP Co affairs), dated 23 Feb 1932.

Folder containing typescript minutes of
meeting of creditors of RMSP Co under
guarantees, on 16 Mar 1932, with another
copy of explanatory memorandum.

Folder containing typescript minutes of
meeting of certain unsecured creditors of
RMSP Co on 16 Mar 1932, with another copy
of explanatory memorandum.

Report of meeting of preference shareholders
in RMSP Co held 12 Feb 1931 with report of
first scheme of arrangement.

Legal Records: Mail contracts, RMSP Co,
admiralty and post office, Vol 1, 1840–76.
(Mainly printed, some typescript and MS
material. Includes mid-nineteenth century
parliamentary papers relating to RMSP mail
contracts); Register of title deeds, 2 vols
1840s–1930s; Register of impressions of
company's seal, 6 vols 1904–49; Folder,
containing agreements between RMSP Co and

Pacific Mail Steam Ship Co and Panama Rail
Road Co. Also schedule, out and home, of
PSN Co through freight rates (1864); Folder
containing duplicated forms with details of
Deeds etc borrowed for use by management
during 1920s; Parcel containing (printed) trust
deeds for securing debenture stocks, 1907,
1910, 1912, 1914(2), 1928 & 1930, and
appointment of new trustees, 1918, 1929(2),
1930; Printed transcript of Rex vs Lord
Kylsant & H.J. Morland. Proceedings at the
Guildhall, London, 2–22 June 1931; Printed
transcript of Rex vs Lord Kylsant & H.J.
Morland. Proceedings at the Old Bailey,
London 20–30 July 1931.

Special committee book (mainly on staff
appointments & salaries), July 1882–July
1903, 1 Vol.

Salaries committee ledgers. 1 Vol, 1903–6,
1 Vol, 1907–15 (marked No 3).

Staff committee. Salary sheets 1912–17, 1 vol

”	”	”	”	1924–8,	1 vol
					(marked No 3)
”	”	”	”	1928–33,	1 vol
					(marked No 4)
”	”	”	” Foreign & Colonial		
		Offices,	1920–31,	1 vol	
					(marked No 1)
”	”	Special salary sheets,			
			1932–58,	1 vol	

Private staff books 1912–30, 4 Vols
Two folders containing complete list of staff
at all offices 25 May 1908 and 21 July 1910
Particulars of staff in all offices, 1 Vol, 1912–19
                              (marked No 4)

Particulars of staff in home offices, 1 Vol, 1924—31

Particulars of staff in offices abroad, 1 Vol, 1923—32

Particulars of staff in home offices, 1 Vol, 1928—40
(marked No 6)

Staff committee: agenda & minute book, 1 Vol 1912—32

Register of temporary staff, 1 Vol, apparently World War I period.

Secretary's (?) memorandum book, containing matters concerned with staff and administration, 1920s.

Register of former employees: Foreign & Colonial Service, 1 Vol, mainly 1920s.

Records of companies associated with RMSP Co
Australasian Pacific Mail Steam Packet Co
Minutes of the court of directors Vol 1, 29 Apl 1852—3 July 1861 (indexed)

Nelson Line (Liverpool) Ltd, and Nelson Steam Navigation Co Ltd
Annual summary (on forms specified in Companies Acts, 1908—17) of capital shares issued, 1920—5.

Private Journal 1 Vol   ) both these are locked volumes
Balance Sheet 1 Vol   ) for which no key is available.

(ii) Items on Permanent Loan to the National Maritime Museum, Greenwich
Reports relative to Smith's Patent Screw Propeller, 1840.

Reproduction of Martin Cortes' Compendium of Navigation.

RMSP Regulations 1850.

Book of Admiralty Instructions for the Crimean War, 1855.

RMSP Petty Cash Account Book 1840—49; Cash Book 1843—44.

Minute book of Provedoring Committee 1854—60

Book of Store Schedules 1902

Details of Service Books (17 vols) 1868—70, 1872—87, 1919—9, 1905—20

Log of RMSP *Clyde* Sept 1846—Jan 1847

Capt D.Symms

PSNC Diary 1913

RMSP Minute Book of Store Committee

RMSP Demi Official Letters 1826—28

RMSP Confidential Letter Book 1876—1908

GPO Daily Packet List 11 July, 1844

Miscellaneous postcards, pamphlets, catalogues; RMSP handbooks, guides, instruction books, etc.

Reports of General Meetings, 1843—1900 (11 volumes); Reports and Accounts, Chairman's speeches.

Papers relating to Stocks and Shares, New York — West Indies Service; Other Services and contracts; General Mail Matters.

Miscellaneous letterbooks, correspondence and files.

4 ACCESS

Enquiries should be addressed to the Librarian, University College, London and to Keeper of Manuscripts, National Maritime Museum. (This handlist was generously compiled by Dr R.S. Craig, Department of History, University College, London and A.W.H. Pearsall, Keeper of Manuscripts, National Maritime Museum.)

WALTER RUNCIMAN & CO LTD

see Moor Line Ltd

CHR SALVESEN & CO (SHIPOWNERS)

1 HISTORY

The business dates from 1843 when Theodor Salvesen, newly arrived from Norway, established a shipping firm in Grangemouth. Three years later he set up a branch in Leith, in the care of a partner George Vair Turnbull. In 1851 Theodor's younger brother Christian Salvesen was brought in from Norway as manager. Both brothers had served an effective commercial apprenticeship in the North Sea trading area. In 1855 Theodor Salvesen withdrew from Leith to concentrate on the Grangemouth business, leaving his brother Christian and Turnbull to set up a new and independent partnership to conduct business based on Leith. The existing records relate to this firm and its successors. When Turnbull withdrew in 1872 Christian Salvesen conducted the firm on his own as C. Salvesen & Co.

In the 1880s he brought his three sons, Thomas, Fred and Theodore into the partnership. From the 1870s the business grew rapidly and diversified, both within shipping and in such activities as timber in North America and coal. Whaling became the most important of these new interests (under Theodore's charge), eventually becoming the most important business of the firm. It was subsequently organised as a separate legal entity, the S. Georgia Co Ltd. Other whaling businesses were incorporated in later years. Whaling was given up in 1964.

2 PRESENT STATUS AND ACTIVITIES

The group now operates as a widely diversified international 'conglomerate' of over thirty companies. Apart from shipping

the firm has interests in food preservation and distribution,
fish meal, construction and other ventures.

3 RECORDS HELD

There are two groups of records: C. Salvesen and T.
Salvesen & Co for
Day books for 1909–15, 1917–41, 1950–53
Ledger, private (TS & Co) for 1867–76
Ledger, private (CS & Co) for 1872–1900
Journal, private (TS & Co) for 1867–78
Journal, private (CS & Co) for 1872–1900
Ledgers for 1888–1929
Cash book (TS & Co) for 1872–76
Cash books (CS & Co) for 1887–1910
Cash books, 1884–90, 1907–46
Petty cash books for 1927–42
Account book, private for 1900–10
Letter books (3) of C. Salvesen for 1857–60,
1870–83
Diary for 1885–98
Diaries of T. Salvesen (13 vols) for 1904–16
Also held are records for the following companies:
Paraffin Oil Co
Ledgers for 1860s–81
Copy letter books for 1862–75
Journals for 1860s–81
South Georgia Co Ltd
Day book No 1909–19
Other financial records:
Polar Whaling Co Ltd
Ledgers for 1930–47
Journals for 1930–47
Accounts for 1948–57
Olna Whaling Co
Day books for 1904–41
Ledgers for 1904–30

Sevilla Whaling Co Ltd
Statement book for 1939—41

4 ACCESS

Some documents are badly damaged by damp. Some are
at Inveralmond House, Cramond, and others at 29 Bernard
Street, Leith. Enquiries may be made to the Secretary,
National Register of Archives (Scotland), PO Box 36, HM
General Register House, Edinburgh 2, mentioning Reference
No NRA (Scot) 0409.

5 REFERENCE

A business history is being prepared by Dr W.
Vamplew, Department of Economic History,
University of Edinburgh.

SILVER LINE LTD

1 HISTORY

The company was founded in 1925.

2 PRESENT STATUS AND ACTIVITIES

The company is a firm of shipowners engaged in world wide
activities.

3 RECORDS HELD

Minute books from 1925
Cash books from 1925
Ledgers from 1925
Contracts for current ships
Technical drawings and blueprints for current
ships, and photographs
Miscellaneous records
The records are in good condition.

4 ACCESS

Access is granted to approved students. Enquiries may be addressed to the Company Secretary, Silver Line Ltd, Palmerston House, 51 Bishopsgate, London EC2.

WILLIAM SLOAN & COMPANY LTD

1 HISTORY

The company was founded in 1955.

2 PRESENT STATUS AND ACTIVITIES

The company is one of shipowners. It is a fully owned subsidiary of Burns & Laird Lines Ltd (since 1 January 1965), which in turn is a subsidiary of Coast Lines Ltd. Business is conducted from Belfast, Bristol, Cardiff and Swansea.

3 RECORDS HELD

Minute books from 1955
Register of directors from 1955
Register of members from 1955
Journals: general from 1960; private from
1955 to 1964
Cash books: general from 1960; private from
1955 to 1964
Ledgers: general from 1960; private from 1955
to 1964
Annual accounts from 1955
Voyage accounts from 1901 to 1954
Letters from 1938 to 1964

4 ACCESS

Enquiries may be addressed to the Company Secretary, William Sloan & Co Ltd, 52 Robertson Street, Glasgow C2.

5 REFERENCE
Duckworth and Langmuir, *op cit*

TYNE-TEES STEAM SHIPPING COMPANY LTD

1 HISTORY

In 1864 a group of well-known Tyneside business men
made arrangements for the formation of a shipping company
which would co-ordinate to a very great extent the coasting
and short sea trade of the port. Thus the Tyne Steam Shipping
Co Ltd came into being. The company took its present title
(Tyne-Tees Steam Shipping Co Ltd) on its amalgamation in
1903 with the Tees Union Shipping Co Ltd. This amalgamation brought under the control of the company the Free
Trade Wharf Co Ltd, London, and through the activities of
this subsidiary business was extended to the trade between
London and the Humber.

Regular services were carried on between Newcastle/Hull/
Middlesbrough/London and also to the Continent, mainly
from the Tyne to Antwerp, Amsterdam, Rotterdam and
Hamburg. An important development occurred in the year
1943 when the company and its subsidiary, Free Trade
Wharf Co Ltd, were acquired by Coast Lines Ltd. The company
also acquired the Aberdeen Steam Navigation Co Ltd in 1945,
which had a considerable trade between Aberdeen and London,
but the trade gradually declined through the effect of road
competition and the company ceased trading in 1964. The
road haulage firm of John Forman Ltd was purchased in
1946 and has made considerable growth since that date.

In 1961 the company acquired T. Roddam Dent & Son Ltd,
wharfingers at Middlesbrough, together with their subsidiary
company, Deepwater Wharf Ltd, Middlesbrough. The wharves
belonging to T. Roddam Dent & Son Ltd co-joined the
company's wharves at Middlesbrough and the purchase thus

gave the company a considerable unbroken wharf frontage. The company also has an investment in the German firm of Continental Seaways GmbH who act as agents for the company's Hamburg trade. The business of stevedoring and wharfage carried on by the company at Middlesbrough was terminated when, by the Tees and Hartlepools Port Authority Act of 1966, all the company's plant and property at Middlesbrough were compulsorily taken over on 1 January 1967.

2 PRESENT STATUS AND ACTIVITIES

The company is one of shipowners, wharfingers and stevedores and is a wholly owned subsidiary of Coast Lines Ltd. Its present activities comprise trading between Middlesbrough, Hull and London, and a regular service from the Tyne to Hamburg and Bremen. A unit load service between Middlesbrough and Rotterdam is run in conjunction with Wm H. Muller & Co (Batavier) NV and a pooling arrangement has also been set up with this firm to deal with the conventional cargo carried by the vessels of each company between Newcastle, Middlesbrough, Antwerp, Amsterdam and Rotterdam.

3 RECORDS HELD

Minute books (6 vols) from 1864 to 1893*
Agenda book (1 vol) from 1903 to 1928*
Reports (drafts) of annual meetings for
1877–1902
Secretarial papers (17 box files) for 1919–43
Monthly profit and loss accounts for 1929–43
Shareholders' instructions (3 vols) for 1872–
1904
Sale and purchase of steamers (5 box files)
for 1930–41
Wages of seamen etc for 1889–91
Contracts for steamers for 1894–5

Collision enquiries for 1883—5 and 1893
Articles of association for 1903
Anglo-Dutch Strawboard and Shipping
Conference 1933—4
Miscellaneous press cuttings and photographs

4 ACCESS
The first two items (marked *) are in the company's offices at 25 King Street, Newcastle-upon-Tyne 1. The remainder are in the Newcastle-upon-Tyne City Archives Office, 7 Saville Place, Newcastle-upon-Tyne 1. Enquiries should be addressed to the City Archivist at this address, mentioning DD 92. No records in this collection less than fifty years old may be shown to the public without permission of the company' secretary.

OTHER KNOWN SHIPPING COMPANY PAPERS

Blue Funnel Line
See sources listed in F.E. Hyde and J.R. Harris, *Blue Funnel* (Liverpool, 1960). The papers of Alfred Holt and George Holt are deposited in the Liverpool Record Office.

C.T. Bowring & Co Ltd
B. Bowring: Ledger, 1830—40; Letter Book, 1840—4; C.T. Bowring: Underwriter's account book 1861—2; C.T. Bowring & Co: account book 1872—80. Deposited in Liverpool Record Office.

British-India Steam Navigation Co
Material is included in the papers of Sir William Mackinnon, deposited in the School of African and Oriental Studies, London, WC1.

Canadian Pacific Line

Records are preserved with a full-time archivist and staff. Enquiries should be addressed to the offices of the company, Montreal, Canada.

Commercial Steam Packet Co (London-Boulogne)

Letters, papers and accounts (1840–4) are deposited in Northumberland County Record Office.

Inman Steamship Co Ltd

Miscellaneous items only, including abstracts of logs and lists of average passengers (nineteenth century) are deposited in Liverpool Record Office.

Okil and Co Ltd

There is a reference to material in Liverpool Record Office.

George Robinson and Co Ltd

There is a reference to material in the Central Library, Manchester.

SECTION II

SHIPPING RECORDS
IN COUNTY AND OTHER
RECORD OFFICES

ABERDEEN UNIVERSITY LIBRARY

Type of Document	Ship's Name	Period Covered	Voyage(s) Made or Port	Master of Ship* or Keeper of Record+ Owner of Ship**
Ref No	Port of Registry		Type of Business	
Journal MS 2070	*Swan* Aberdeen	5–8 Dec 1788	Aberdeen – Gravesend	Dr J. Troup+
	Duchess of Portland	29 Dec 1788–11 May 1789	Gravesend – Dominica	Dr J Troup+ Capt Francis*
" MS 2238	*Christian* Aberdeen	1791	Northern waters; whaling	G. Kerr+
" MS 2137		1833–4	UK – Canada	P. Bell+
" Letters MS 2526	*Scotia* Banff	1878–93		W. Duncan* Mrs I. Duncan+
Accounts MS 2295		1842–4		Capt W. Penny+
" MS 2415	*Terra Nova*	18 Aug 1903–18 Aug 1904	Antarctica	W.C. Souter+
	Note: Ship's surgeon, HM Antarctic Relief Ship; receipts and issues of medicines.			
Misc		1842–4		Capt W. Penny+

Access Apply to: University Librarian, King's College, Aberdeen.
Opening hours: Mon – Fri 9–5; Sat 9–1.

BEDFORD COUNTY RECORD OFFICE

Minute Book X52/86		1797–9		
	Note: Committee of merchants, shipowners, insurers and inhabitants of London to counteract mutiny at the Nore.			

Access Apply to: County Archivist, Bedford County Record Office,
Shire Hall, Bedford.
Opening hours: Mon – Fri 9.15–1, 2–5; Sat 9.15–12.15
(in summer by appointment)

BERKSHIRE RECORD OFFICE

Type of Document	Ship's Name	Period Covered	Voyage(s) Made or Port	Master of Ship* or Keeper of Record+ Owner of Ship**
Ref No	Port of Registry		Type of Business	
Log Book D/EPg	*Parana*	2 July—17 Oct 1859	West Indies	T.A. Bevis* W.H. Pinniger+
	,,	7 Dec 1864—2 Jan 1865	S America (Rio)	,,
	,,	9 Feb—5 Apr 1865	,,	,,
	,,	10 Apr—4 June 1865	,,	R. Woolward* W.H. Pinniger+
	Clyde	8 Nov 1859—22 Feb 1860	West Indies	J. Mott (?)* W.H. Pinniger+
	Thames	6 Dec 1860—13 Feb 1861	West Indies (St Thomas)	A. Hole (?)* W.H. Pinniger+
	Seine	13 Feb—28 Apr 1861		R. Revett* W.H. Pinniger+
	Oneida	10 May—3 July 1861	S America	T.A. Bevis* W.H. Pinniger+
	Magdalena	9 Dec 1863—6 Jan 1864	,, (Rio)	R. Curlewis* W.H. Pinniger+
	Mersey	7 Jan-9 July 1864	,, (Rio)	,,
		10 July—6 Dec 1864	,,	,,
	Note: Pinniger's service was with the Royal Mail Steam Packet Co (W Indies and S American services).			
Journal D/EDB1		1623—38	East Indies, Spain	A London merchant
Ledger D/EDB2		,,	,,	A London (?) merchant+
D/EEZ31		1707—9		,,

Type of Document / Ref No	Ship's Name / Port of Registry	Period Covered	Voyage(s) Made or Port / Type of Business	Master of Ship* or Keeper of Record+ Owner of Ship**
Accounts (shares in ships & cargoes)				
D/EByB20		1727		
D/EByA142		1733–40		
D/EByB7		1744	India	
D/EByB1, 2, 6		1764–82		E India Company**
Bills of sale of shares D/ESv(M) F10		1753–62		
Petitions Trumbull Add.MSS37	c 1620– c 1700			
Note: To Privy Council etc on trade and shipping.				
Conveyance D/EDF33	*Eagle*	1626		
Note: Of one third part in ship.				
Insurance policies & bonds D/ESv(M) F7, 8, 10		1744–63	East Indies	
D/EHyB5		1782	London – Portsmouth	
Deed of sale D/ELbT17	*Commodore* London	1847		
Investigation proceedings D/P113/ 28/3	*Hardy*	1861		
Note: Enquiry into loss of ship.				
Assignment D/EBuT97	*Booth*	1754		
Agreement for voyage D/EDF32	*Planter*	1622	Virginia	
Apprenticeship indentures D/EX23 F1, 2		1752, 1776	Rochester	

Type of Document	Ship's Name	Period Covered	Voyage(s) Made or Port	Master of Ship* or Keeper of Record+ Owner of Ship**
Ref No	Port of Registry		Type of Business	
Charter-parties D/EKmB2,	Hamilton Galley	1724, 1734	Slave trade	
Corres misc D/EBuF13 D/EHyF86 D/EHy017/ 3 D/EDC72 D/EX23F 31/4		1648–52 1778 1782 early 19th century 1924		
Bills of Lading D/EPbE86, 87 D/EHyB4/1 D/EHyA10/ 2		1700–10 1775 1780	Bristol Hull	

Access: Apply to: County Archivist, Berkshire Record Office, Shire Hall, Reading.

Opening hours: Mon, Tues, Wed, Fri, 9–5.30; Thurs 9–7.30.

BRISTOL ARCHIVES

Acct Bk	Snow Fanny	1777–89	Baltic	Capt Olive*
12162	Bristol		Barbados	T. Richards*
			Trading and slaving	J.P. Devenish*

Note: This volume covers twelve voyages and comprises copies of sailing instructions, accounts for equipping and provisioning the ship, portledge bill, manifests of cargo and final balance sheets. Owners: S. Munckley, R. Twine, G. Gibbs, T.G.J. Richards.

Access   Apply to: Archivist, Bristol Archives Office, The Council House, Bristol 1.

Opening hours: Mon – Fri 9–5; Sat 9–12.

BRISTOL CITY MUSEUM

Type of Document	Ship's Name	Period Covered	Voyage(s) Made or Port	Master of Ship* or Keeper of Record+
Ref No	Port of Registry		Type of Business	Owner of Ship**
Log Acct No 7218 Reg No J142	*Great Western* Bristol	2 Apr—May 1842	Bristol — New York — Bristol	J. Hosken*
Acct Bk	*Snow Africa*	1776	New Calabar	G. Merrick*
Ref No 2404	Bristol		Old Calabar trading and slaving	T. Baker*
Access	Apply to: City Librarian, City Museum & Library, Queens Road, Bristol 8.			

BRISTOL REFERENCE LIBRARY

Log	*Great Western* Bristol	8 Apr—17 May 1838	Bristol—New York	Lt Hosken* RN Chief Engineer+
	Great Western	25 July—4 Sep 1846	Liverpool — New York	Chief Engineer+
Journal B 4764	*Black Prince* Bristol	24 Apr 1762— 19 Dec 1764	Bristol — Gold Coast Trading and slaving	M. Laroche* Mate +
Ledger B21256	*Tryall* Bristol	11 July 1757— 30 Aug 1760		H. Bright+
Ledger (extracts) B21258	*Sybil* *Success*	1779—86	Bristol — West India	T. Weekes* W. Mettocks* W. Ball* Various hands+
	and other documents			
Access	Apply to: City Librarian, Central Library, College Green, Bristol 1.			
	Opening hours: Mon — Sat 9—5.			

BUCKINGHAMSHIRE RECORD OFFICE

Type of Document	Ship's Name	Period Covered	Voyage(s) Made or Port	Master of Ship* or Keeper of Record+
Ref No	Port of Registry		Type of Business	Owner of Ship**
Accounts	*Prosperous*	1665–1671		
D/LE/15/7	*Sarah*	,, ,,		

Access	Apply to: County Archivist, Buckinghamshire Record Office, County Hall, Aylesbury, Bucks.
	Opening hours: Mon – Fri 9.15–1, 2–5.30.

CAMBRIDGESHIRE AND ISLE OF ELY COUNTY RECORD OFFICE

Type of Document	Ship's Name	Period Covered	Voyage(s) Made or Port	Master of Ship
Journal R57/24/– /21/1(c)	*Essex*	29 June – 29 Sep 1841	Portsmouth – Madras	Lt E. Green+
Journal R58/8/– /14/18	*Shannon; Maria-Pia*	9 Oct 1867 Nov 1867	Southampton – Lisbon-Madeira	Miss E.H.J. Beldam+
Journal 279/F2	*Lusitania*	16 Dec 1877– 22 Jan 1878	St Vincent – Adelaide – Melbourne (Australia)	J.M. Holworthy+
Bill of sale (share)	*Mary* Kings Lynn	1836		
Corres- pondence	various ships			J. Thorp et al

Access	Apply to: County Archivist, Cambridge and Isle of Ely Record Office, Shire Hall, Castle Hill, Cambridge.
	Opening hours: Mon – Fri 9–1, 1.45–5.30.

CORNWALL COUNTY RECORD OFFICE

Type of Document	Ship's Name	Period Covered	Voyage(s) Made or Port
Log Book	*Guiding Star*	Oct 1884 – Feb 1885	Mediterranean – England
AD71/18	Padstow		London – Newport

Type of Document Ref No	Ship's Name Port of Registry	Period Covered	Voyage(s) Made or Port Type of Business	Master of Ship* or Keeper of Record+ Owner of Ship**
		Apr 1887 Apr 1888	Fecamp Weston Dock toward Iceland; fish, liquor	
Account Book DDRG1/17	*Magic*	1833–1839	Italy, Syria, Smyrna Danzig Constantinople	Capt C. Trewavas
"	*Chyandour*	1842–1850	Cornwall–Wales	Capt Jn Hain+ B. Bukerley+
Access	Apply to: County Archivist, County Hall, Truro, Cornwall. Opening hours: Mon–Fri 9–1; 2.15–5; Sat 9–12.30.			

CUMBERLAND WESTMORLAND AND CARLISLE RECORD OFFICE

Log book D/BS	*Earl of Abergavenny*	Mar 1799–Oct 1800	China	J. Words-worth*+ E.India Co**
D/Sen	*Rose*	Mar 1828–Aug 1829	Madras and Bengal	T.Marquis* East India Co** J.A. Senhouse+
Log book (copy) D/Da/33	*Aimwell* Whitehaven	Jan–Feb 1836	Bahia	D. Power*
Account book (supplies etc) D/Ben	*Eleanor* Whitehaven	1762–71	Dublin, Liverpool Christiansand 1763; Virginia 1763; Amsterdam, St Petersburg 1765; North America 1767 1771	
Account books	*Earl of Abergavenny*	1783–1800	China	J. Words-worth*+

Type of Document	Ship's Name	Period Covered	Voyage(s) Made or Port	Master of Ship* or Keeper of Record+ Owner of Ship**
Ref No	Port of Registry		Type of Business	
(personal and trading) D/BS	*Earl of Sandwich*	1783–84	China	J. Words-worth*+
Access	Apply to: Archivist, Cumberland, Westmorland and Carlisle Record Office, The Castle, Carlisle, and County Hall, Kendal.			
	Opening hours: Mon – Fri 9–5; Sat by arrangement.			

DEVON RECORD OFFICE

Diary 877M/F1	*Selkirk-shire*	1882	Queensland Carrying Emigrants	Mrs F. Thornton+
	Note: wife of ship's medical officer.			
Access	Apply to: County Archivist, Devon Record Office, County Hall, Topsham Road, Exeter, Devon.			
	Opening hours: Mon–Fri 9.15– 5.15; Sat morning by arrangement.			

DORSET RECORD OFFICE

Bill of Sale D203/A31 D203/A45 "	*John and Samuel Edgar Othello Desdemona*	1752 1782 1875 "		
Access	Apply to: County Archivist, Dorset Record Office, County Hall, Dorchester.			
	Opening hours: Mon – Fri 9–1, 2–5 (Mon to 5.30).			

Access	Apply to: County Archivist, Durham Co Record Office, County Hall, Durham.
	Opening hours: Mon — Fri 8.30—5.

ESSEX RECORD OFFICE

Type of Document	Ship's Name	Period Covered	Voyage(s) Made or Port	Master of Ship* or Keeper of Record+ Owner of Ship**
Ref No.	Port of Registry		Type of Business	
Log	*Kalgan*	1 Feb—27 June 1917	Tientsin — Hong Kong	Capt H.E. Laver*+ China Navigation Co**

Access	Apply to: County Archivist, Essex Record Office, County Hall, Chelmsford, Essex.
	Opening hours: Mon 9.15—8.45; Tue — Fri 9.15—5.15.

EXETER CITY LIBRARY

Log Book Holman bequest	*Eagle* Topsham	1711—12	Topsham — Virginia	J. Chappel* ,, +
,,	*Townsend*	1716—18	England — Canton	C. Kessor* D. Ireson+
,,	*Patience and Judith*	1718—19	Boston, Mass	J. Osborne*
,,	*Mountague*	1719—20	Deptford — Canton	
,,	*Brothers*	1804—6	England — India — Madagascar; Whaling	R. Bagwell* ,, +
,,	*Fanny*	1807—8	River Plate — England	R. Bagwell*+
		1808—9	England — Portugal	,,
,,	*Miss Platoff*	1813—14	Portsmouth — St John's, Newfoundland; Portugal; Trading	,, *+ R. Bagwell
,,	*Flora*	1817	Topsham — Porto	R. Bagwell*
,,	*Symmetry*	1819—20	London — Naples — Palermo — Rio — London	R. Bagwell+

DURHAM COUNTY RECORD OFFICE

Type of Document Ref No	Ship's Name Port of Registry	Period Covered	Voyage(s) Made or Port Type of Business	Master of Ship* or Keeper of Record+ Owner of Ship**

General information	The two main holdings are
	  (a) Papers of Joseph Brown, master mariner for Taylor & Sanderson Steamship Co Ltd, Sunderland (D/X 73) and
	  (b) Papers relating to steamships owned by Lord Londonderry (D/LOB 388-916)			

Accounts, wages D/X 73	*Universal*	1902–10		
Portage books (3 vols) D/X 73	*Universal* *Britannia* *Alexandra* *Thornhill* *Neilrose* *Vaux* *Andelle* *Nivelle* *Ravonia* *Lancing*	1907–25		
Letter books (4 vols)	*Universal* *Britannia* *Alexandra* *Thornhill* *Neilrose* *Vaux* *Andelle*	1908–16, 1919–23		
Agreement charter	*Peeress*	1905		
,, *Inventory*	*Sunderland* *Warshark*	c 1915		
Plans D/AP	various vessels	19th-20th centuries		Austin & Pickersgill Ltd, Sunderland
D/X 73	*Thornhill* *Peeress*	c 1810–1900 ,, ,,		
Miscellaneous papers D/X73 and D/LOB 388-416				

Type of Document Ref No	Ship's Name Port of Registry	Period Covered	Voyage(s) Made or Port Type of Business	Master of Ship* or Keeper of Record+ Owner of Ship**
Holman bequest	*Symmetry*	1820–1	Valparaiso – Montevideo – Liverpool	
,,	*William*	1822	Liverpool – Bristol waters (coasting)	R. Bagwell*+ R. Bagwell*
Ledger		1754–9	Exeter Whale Fishing Co	
Exeter City Archives				
Ledgers, Letter-book, Account books etc Holman bequest		1845–95	J. Holman & Sons shipowners	
Account books(5) Holman bequest		1809–26		Capt R. Bagwell
Account book Holman bequest	*Band of Hope*	1860–70		Capt Symonds
Apportion-ment books (2)		1860–7	Neptune Shipping Average Insurance Association	
Access	Apply to: City Librarian, Exeter City Library, Castle Street, Devon.			
	Opening hours: Mon – Fri 10–5.30; Sat 9.30–12.30.			

FLINTSHIRE RECORD OFFICE

Log books (2) Acc.679	*Viola* Whitehaven	1890–9		
papers, various	,,	1872–1916		
Access	Apply to: County Archivist, Flintshire Record Office, The Old Rectory, Hawarden, Nr Chester.			
	Opening hours: Mon – Fri 9.30–1, 2–5; Sat 9.30–12.			

GATESHEAD PUBLIC LIBRARY

Type of Document Ref No	Ship's Name Port of Registry	Period Covered	Voyage(s) Made or Port Type of Business	Master of Ship* or Keeper of Record+ Owner of Ship**
Bills of Sale	*Susanna* Newcastle	1694 1698		
Cotes-worth MSS	*Reserve* Shields	1702		

Access Apply to: Borough Librarian, Central Library, Prince Consort Road, Gateshead 8, Co Durham.

Opening hours: Mon — Sat 10—8 (5 Wed & Sat)

GLAMORGAN COUNTY RECORD OFFICE

Ref No	Ship's Name / Port	Period Covered	Voyage/Business	Master/Owner
Log book Q/S Misc D/DNHA 99	*Isabella* Guernsey *Gipsy*	1851—2 1909—18, 1922	Guernsey—Corunna Cardiff Corunna; Coal, cattle towing, Neath	I. Jones* M. Godkin+
Ledger D/DNHA 98	"	1899—1926	"	
Account Book D/DMa192	*Capricorn*	1847—62		L.R. Fitz-maurice+
D/DP 887	*Gulliver* Swansea	1844—61	Welsh ports, Bristol; coal, culm, limestone, brick	W. Bevan*
D/DXeo 78	*Victoria* Aberayron	1843—7	Welsh ports; wool culm, limestone	J. Jones*
D/DXeo 79	*Puella* Aberayron	1873—9, 1896	Welsh, English, Continental ports	
D/DXeo 80	*Kilmeny* Glasgow	1915—16	Belfast—New York Adelaide, Fremantle	J. Davies*
Cash book D/DNHa 100	*Gipsy*	1899—1934	towing, Neath	

Type of Document Ref No	Ship's Name Port of Registry	Period Covered	Voyage(s) Made or Port Type of Business	Master of Ship* or Keeper of Record+ Owner of Ship**
Corres-pondence Accounts etc D/DX qc 13	*Kara* Cardiff "	1838	Liverpool—Cork—Haiti; coffee	J.B. Barber*
		1839	Palermo—Messina—London	C.H. Louttid*
	"	1840	London—Sicily	"
	"	1841	Sicily—London	C.H. Louttid, C.Skirling*
	"	"	Naples—Sicily—Liverpool	
	"	1842	Liverpool—Mediterranean	C.Skirling*
	"	1843	Leghorn—British ports—Smyrna—British ports	"
	"	1844	Rotterdam—French and British port (wrecked)	W.Skirling*
Registers of shipping (3 vls) D/DT 1265—7		1833—8, 1837—41 1897—1901		
Plans and drawings D/DNAI		c 1810—80	38 vessels built at Neath Abbey Ironworks	
Miscell-aneous D/DGN/E 196-205	*Charlott* Neath	1780		
	Caterina	1781		

Note: Account of wrecks.

Access   Apply to: County Archivist, Glamorgan County Record Office, County Hall, Catheys Park, Cardiff.

Opening hours: Mon — Fri 9—5.

GLASGOW CITY ARCHIVES

Account book B1.18.11 Passenger Lists	*Isabella*	Aug 1829—Mar 1832	Antigua, Rio, Hamburg	A. Duncan or Mac-Donald*
		1871—80		P. Hender-son & Co**

Access   Apply to: Archivist, PO Box 27, City Chambers, Glasgow C1.

Opening hours: Mon — Fri 9—5, by appointment.

GLOUCESTER CITY LIBRARY

Type of Document	Ship's Name	Period Covered	Voyage(s) Made or Port	Master of Ship* or Keeper of Record+
Ref No	Port of Registry		Type of Business	Owner of Ship**
Log (Stevenson) 1694	*Hanna Eastee* Liverpool	29 June 1861– 29 Mar 1862	New York – Havana Havana – New York	W.L.Brown* R. Thompson*
			New York – Gloucester; machinery, grain	
1695	*Leander* Padstow	2 May 1866– 11 Jan 1867	Liverpool Malta, (coal) Malta – (ballast; Bordeaux (staves) Bordeaux – Gloucester (grain, staves)	R. Seargent* G.H.Moses+
Access	Apply to: City Librarian, Gloucester City Library, Brunswick Road, Gloucester. Opening hours: Mon – Fri 9–8.30; Sat 9–7			

GLOUCESTERSHIRE RECORD OFFICE

Log D1439	*Hillsborough*	1793–4	London–Bengal –London	East India** E. Brown*
Log D1292 (Acc 2010)	*William Fairlie* London	1829–34	London–Bengal– Penang–Singapore –China–St Helena –Gravesend	J. Tombes+ Co T. Blair* G. Gordon*
Journal D543 (Acc 226)	*Sarah and Elizabeth* Hull	1836–7	London – S. Australia Whaling	S. Australian Co.** Wakeling* G.E. Stranger+ S. Australian Co.**
,,	*Solway*	1837	Australian waters whaling	G.E. Stranger+
,,	*Seppings*	1838	Hobart–Cape Horn –The Downs	S. Australian Co.** G.E. Stranger+

Type of Document Ref No	Ship's Name Port of Registry	Period Covered	Voyage(s) Made or Port Type of Business	Master of Ship* or Keeper of Record+ Owner of Ship**
Corres-pondence D/33/378-9	*Colchester*	1702	to Fort St George	E India Co** P.Wyrhall+
,, D48/C2, C4, C7-9, C10		1821—59		

Note: between Mr Henwood, patentee of 'dead eye' rigging device, to Capt H.J. and Anne Huntley.

Legal Papers D1799/T3		1582		

Note: Declaration of acquittal of charges of piracy against J. Wynter during Francis Drake's circumnavigation of the world.

Plan and descrip-tion Hyett pamphlets		1737		

Note: Machine for carrying vessels into or out of harbour, etc by J. Hulls.

Access Apply to: Record Office, Gloucestershire Record Office, Shire Hall, Gloucester.

Opening hours: Mon — Fri 9—12.45, 1.45—5, Sat by arrangement.

GREATER LONDON RECORD OFFICE

General Information The minutes of the council (LCC and GLC) and its committees contain references to various vessels owned by the council, including Woolwich Ferry vessels, river steamboats for 1905-7, and various sludge vessels, of which the most important are listed below.

Logs, Masters & Engineers			
	John Perring	Nov 1949—Jul 1963	Beckton, Crossness
		Apr 1950—May 1959	Black Deep, Thames Estuary
	J.H. Hunter	Jun 1950—Nov 1965	(sludge vessels)
		Sep 1949—May 1966	
	Henry Ward	Jan 1950—Sep 1957	
	,, ,,	Nov 1949—Sep 1957	
	Edward Cruse	Jul 1954—Jan 1966	
	,,	Jul 1954—Nov 1965	

Type of Document	Ship's Name	Period Covered	Voyage(s) Made or Port	Master of Ship* or Keeper of Record+ Owner of Ship**
	Port of Registry		Type of Business	
Log	*Sir Joseph Bazalgette*	Nov 1963–Jan 1966 Apr 1964–Jan 1966 Nov 1963	Greenock–London	
Insurance policy O/140/12	*Morse*	1775	Malacca–Canton–London	
,, Q/UL/D/Z1	*Elizabeth*	1818		
Bill of Sale BRH/685/1/73	*Loyal Subject*	1680		
Apprenticeship Indenture BRA/717/3/1	*Sir Andrew Hammond*	1828		
BRA/717/3/2,3	*Perseverance*	1829		
BRA/717/3/4	*Sering-apatam*	1831		
	Note: To W. Mellish, shipowner			
Mortgage O/35/68	*Harmony* Rochester	1829		
Letters, patent assignment of BRA/329/X/4		1844	Invention of improvement in working ships chain	
Access	Apply to: Head Archivist and Librarian, Greater London Record Office, County Hall, London SE1. Opening hours: Mon – Fri 9.45–4.45, Sat by arrangement.			

GREAT YARMOUTH BOROUGH RECORDS

Log	*Albert*	1892–4	Yarmouth – Newfoundland	J.F. Trezise*+
D24/67	Great Yarmouth		Yarmouth – Manchester; Swansea–Labrador	

Type of Document	Ship's Name	Period Covered	Voyage(s) Made or Port	Master of Ship* or Keeper of Record+ Owner of Ship**
	Port of Registry		Type of Business	
Journals		1730–55	Europe, North and South America, India	J. Secker
Bills of sale	various vessels	1823–54		
Bills of fare	*Clyde*	1867–70	to Calcutta, troops	
Access	Apply to: Borough Archivist, County Borough of Great Yarmouth, Town Clerk's Department, Town Hall, Great Yarmouth.			
	Opening hours: Mon – Fri 8.30–5.30.			

GUILDFORD MUNIMENT ROOM

Accounts 120/3/11	*Tinmouth Castle*	1776–77	Tynemouth– London, coal	
Insurance records LM 1087/ 1,2,21		1691–93		
	Note: List of ships insured by T. Molyneux.			
Access	Apply to: Archivist, Guildford Muniment Room, Castle Arch, Guildford.			
	Opening hours: Mon–Sat 9–5, preferably by appointment.			

HAMPSHIRE RECORD OFFICE

Journal 15M50/ 1574	*Duff* Portsmouth?	14 Dec 1798 – 8 Jan 1799	London – Montevideo, Rio de la Plata	Capt R. Robson A Missionary
Account Books	*Diana?*	1805	Southampton – Cornwall	W. Waller*
Bills of Sale	*Diana*	1799, 1809		
Access	Apply to: County Archivist, Hampshire Record Office, The Castle, Winchester.			
	Opening hours: Mon – Fri 9.30–5.			

HERTFORDSHIRE COUNTY RECORD OFFICE

Type of Document	Ship's Name Port of Registry	Period Covered	Voyage(s) Made or Port Type of Business	Master of Ship* or Keeper of Record+ Owner of Ship**
Journal AG1005	*General Barker*	1780	Madras — Madagascar — St Helena—England	A. Tod* Sir T. Rumbold+ E India Co**
Journal 25929	*Dublin*	1789	Bengal—London	T. Calvert+ E India Co**
	Note: Also description of St Helena, ref 25930 A.C			
Journal AR942	*Australia*	1880	Southampton— India	W.Grimston+ P & O Line**
Account book (3) GH 1675-7	*General Coote*	1782—4	Gravesend—Madras —China—Macao— Gravesend	R.Williams+ (ship's owner)
Accounts F842	*Tainui*	1893	England — S Africa	Mrs C. Hambury+
Access	Apply to: County Archivist, Herts Record Office, County Hall, Hertford, Herts. Opening hours: Mon — Fri 9.15 — 1; 2—5.15.			

IPSWICH & EAST SUFFOLK RECORD OFFICE

Logs FC 184 /N1/1	*Merope*	13 Mar 1825— 18 Jan 1827	India, China, Sandwich Is California	
HA61:436 /355	*Jannet*	1 Oct 1844— 5 Mar 1845	London — Mauritius	J.Chalmers* C.A. Broke+
HA61:436 /356	*Maidstone*	22 Mar — 25 May 1846	Cape of Good Hope—London	C.A. Broke+
HD49:405 /95	*Spider* Lowestoft	1889—92		
Letter bk EE1/01/1	Various of Aldeburgh	1625—63		
Letter HA2/A2 /1/31	*Britannia*	27 Oct 1829		G. Bayley+
HA13/G /10	*Harry Kelly*	nd	Newcastle — Scarborough	B. Jowel+

Type of Document	Ship's Name	Period Covered	Voyage(s) Made or Port	Master of Ship* or Keeper of Record
	Port of Registry		Type of Business	Owner of Ship**
Account books HA28:50 /23/1.10 (1)-(19)	*Enterprise*	1813—22 1833—4	Coastal ,,	Mingaye Rope
	Sophia	1836—70	,,	of Orford**
	Idas	1827—43	,,	,,
	Idas: Ann	1843—50	,,	,,
	Coaster	1839—70	,,	,,
	Clementina	1834—70	,,	,,
	Ann Queen	1828—48	,,	,,
	Adelaide	1834—53	,,	,,
	Perseverance	1824—46	,,	,,
HA28:50 /23/1.10 (20)-(25)	*Dorothea Economy;*	1830—60	,,	,,
	Lucy	1825—35	,,	,,
	Gainsborough	1825—9	,,	,,
	Commercial Packet	1830—40	,,	,,
	Plough	1839—57	,,	,,
Cargo books HA28:50 /23/1.11 (1)-(3)	*Ann*	1838—50	Coastal	Mingaye Rope**
	Enterprise	1843—6	,,	,,
	Plough	1843—6	,,	,,
	Clementina	c 1858	,,	,,
Profit or loss a/c HA28:50 /23/1.6 (3)	ships above and *Providence*	1831—43	,,	,, ,,
	also correspondence of Mingaye & Rope			
Day Book S1/2/102	*Amy; American*	1765—89		
Papers, Accounts S1/2/104	*Walmer Castle; Earl St Vincent*	1795—1801		
HB1/36A /1/9-11	*Fern*	1863—5		
Voucher HA49:331 Box 19	*Dudley Orford*	1721—32		R. Lashley*
Crew list accts FC184/ N1/10	*Merope*	1829		
Diary HA61:436 /360	*Lord Warden*	6 Feb — 6 Apr 1877	London — Australia	W.C. Loraine+

Type of Document	Ship's Name	Period Covered	Voyage(s) Made or Port	Master of Ship* or Keeper of Record+ Owner of Ship**
	Port of Registry		Type of Business	
Note bk HA61:436 /357	*Ava;* *Hindostan;* *Pottinger*	1856 1856 1856	Southampton — India	W.C. Loraine+ "
Letters HB1/5A /1/1.33	*Umbilo* *Umzinto*	26 March 1891 — 2 May 1895	UK — India — S Africa	R.A. Horn+
Purser's Bond S1/1/ 77.38	*Beaver* London	1637	To Spain & France	
Partnership S1/1/ 77.42	*Seatrade* London	1637	Archangel	
Receipt on a/c S1/1/ 77.64	*Good Success*	17th century	Russia	
Inventory HA30:50 /22/4.2	*Friends Adventure* Southwold	1706		
Protest EL1:2925 /3081-2	*Mary*	1848		
EL1:2925/ 2650-2668 3080	*Lady Leighton;* *Oscar*	1850		
Receipt of wages AX1/7	*Le Michel* Ipswich	1311		
Insurance K10/1/1.4	*Competitor* Maldon	1881	with Ipswich Maritime Association Ltd	E. Tovee*
S1/13/6.1	*True Briton*	1764		Harrison*
Bills of sale HA145: 2940-1	*Wanata* Liverpool *Eveline* Quebec *Orwell* Ipswich *Thomas and Mary*	1853 1854—5 1832 1778		
HD83:995	*Hawk* Yarmouth	1834		
X1/8/2.2	*The Honour* Ipswich	1730		

Type of Document	Ship's Name Port of Registry	Period Covered	Voyage(s) Made or Port Type of Business	Master of Ship* or Keeper of Record+ Owner of Ship**
S1/1 77.45	Samuel London	1638		
S1/1/ 77.53	Swiftsure London	1641		J. Driver*
W3/2/1.1 -1.5	Industry; Prince of Orange	1767–75		
W3/2/1.6	William and Mary	1741		
W3/2/1.7	Norfolk	1778		
W/3/2/1.8	Draper	1782		
Ha18/GA/1	Betty London	1689		J. Tucker*
HA18/GA/2	British Merchant	1715		T. Gilbert*
HA18/GA/3	Sunderland Frigot	1717–18		R. Brown*
S1/1/35.3	Elizabeth Wivenhoe	1671		
S1/1/35.4 35.5	John and Richard Wivenhoe	1672		
S1/1/35.11	John and Andrew Colchester	1680		
HD22:52 /16/40	Johnny and Betsy Southwold	1755		J. Julians*
HB26:412 /1552	Norfolk Southwold	1848	(Copy)	J. Soans*
Bargain and sale HA1/GA/ 3/12	Ambrose; John; Theodosia; Crowley	1740	N America HM Service	W. Smaler* R. Clarke*
HA1/GA/ 4/4	Ambrose Theodosia Mary	1756		
HA1/BE/ 1/5	Constant James Woodbridge Constant Richard Ipswich	1682–3		Withe*

Type of Document Port of Registry	Ship's Name	Period Covered	Voyage(s) Made or Port Type of Business	Master of Ship* or Keeper of Record+ Owner of Ship**
Covenant for sale T4/18/1	Dove Woodbridge Mary Ann Woodbridge	1675—6		
Papers HA128: 2663	Thomas and Ann	1846		G. Worlidge*
	Speedwell	1843		R. Francis*
	Heart of Oak Ipswich	1842		J. Newson*

Access Apply to: Archivist, Ipswich and East Suffolk Record Office, County Hall, Ipswich.

Opening hours: Mon — Fri 9.15—6; Sats by arrangement.

KENT COUNTY ARCHIVES

Type of Document Port of Registry	Ship's Name	Period Covered	Voyage(s) Made or Port / Type of Business	Master of Ship* or Keeper of Record+ Owner of Ship**
Log Marsham Mss U1121 07		1623—5	to Tierra del Fuego and Peru	

Note: kept for Lord L'Hermite; Dutch voyage to conquer Peru; long account of Tierradelfuego

Type of Document Port of Registry	Ship's Name	Period Covered	Voyage(s) Made or Port / Type of Business	Master of Ship* or Keeper of Record+ Owner of Ship**
Log Sackville Mss U269 F42	Harriet	1852	Quebec—London	
Letter book C2/40	New London	1677—1706	England—India	J. Daniel+
Shipping lists Sa/Z23/ 25-29		late 16th century	Ramsgate— Yarmouth Sandwich—Walmer	
Minute Books 3 vols	Virginia	1655		
Letter books Banks Mss U234 B1-3	Dethick			
Order book Stebbing bequest U924 Z1		1771—91	Unnamed firm of boat builders at Deal	

Type of Document	Ship's Name / Port of Registry	Period Covered	Voyage(s) Made or Port / Type of Business	Master of Ship* or Keeper of Record+ Owner of Ship**
Accounts Sa/FUp 1		1823–36	Sandwich Borough Pavement commissioners	
Legal records CPw/A		1632–1906	Lord Warden's courts, register of Cinque Port; mainly salvage	
CPw/L		1496–1852	Court of Lodemanage fellowship of Cinque Port pilots	
(register of Affidavits) Sa/AH/7	various vessels from Sandwich etc	1749–1802		
Miscellaneous Fa/Z17		1762–5, 1793	Coastal trade from Faversham, Whitstable and Herne Bay	
Access	Apply to: County Archivist, Kent Archives Office, County Hall, Maidstone, Kent.			
	Opening hours: Mon – Fri 9–5.15; Sat by arrangement.			

LANCASHIRE RECORD OFFICE

Journals and logs DD BB 8/4	*Reserve* Liverpool	22 June – 1 Aug 1688	Barbados – London	C. Moore* B. Blundell+
"	"	6 Nov 1690– 14 Feb 1691	Liverpool – Virginia	"
		2 May – 30 Aug 1691	Virginia – Lancaster	"
		14 Oct – 15 Dec 1692	Liverpool – Monseratt	W. Webster* B. Blundell+
		16 Jan – 3 Aug 1693	Monserrat – Liverpool	L. Jenkin*
	Amettey Liverpool	5 Jan 1693/4 – 18 Feb 1693/4	Liverpool – Virginia	"
		10 May–27 June 1694	Cape Henrey, Virginia – Liverpool	B. Blundell+

Type of Document	Ship's Name / Port of Registry	Period Covered	Voyage(s) Made or Port / Type of Business	Master of Ship* or Keeper of Record+ Owner of Ship**
Journals and logs DD BB 8/4	*Amettey* Liverpool	22 Nov 1694 – 9 Feb 1695	Liverpool – Virginia	B. Blundell+ L. Jenkins*
,,	,,	17 June – 31 July 1695	Virginia – Liverpool	B. Blundell+
,,	,,	11 Feb 1695/6– 4 Apr 1696	Liverpool – Virginia	,,
,,	,,	10 July–13 Sept 1696	Virginia – Liverpool	,,
	Mulberry Liverpool	26 Jan 1696/7 – 25 Mar 1697	Liverpool – Virginia	,,
,,		7 May – 3 July 1697	Virginia – Liverpool	,,
,,	*Mulberry* Liverpool	9 Nov 1697–17 June 1698	Liverpool – Virginia Liverpool	,, B. Blundell*
,,	,,	13 Oct 1698 – 30 May 1689	,,	B. Blundell+
,,	,,	9 Nov 1699 – 13 June 1700	,,	,,
,,	,,	22 Nov 1701 – 16 July 1701	,,	,,
,,	*Lever* Virginia	24 Sept 1701 – 14 July 1702	Liverpool – Dublin – Barbados – Virginia – Liverpool –	,,
,,	,,	5 Oct 1702 – 26 May 1703	Liverpool – Virginia – Liverpool	,,
,,	,,	Sep 1703 – Oct 1704	,,	,,
,,	,,	Jan 1704/5 – Oct 1705	,,	,,
,,	,,	Jan 1705/6 – Jan 1706/7	,,	,,
,,	*Endeavour*	31 Mar – 9 June 1707	Liverpool – Philadelphia	,, E. Tarleton*
,,	*Cleveland*	19 June 1707 – 20 Mar 1707/8	Philadelphia – Liverpool	B. Blundell+
,,	,,	7 Oct 1708 – 17 Apr 1709	Liverpool – Virginia – Liverpool	,,
,,	,,	17 July – 23 Aug 1709	Liverpool – Archangel	B. Blundell+
,,	,,	9 Sept – 21 Oct 1709	Archangel Liverpool	,,

Type of Document	Ship's Name / Port of Registry	Period Covered	Voyage(s) Made or Port / Type of Business	Master of Ship* or Keeper of Record+ Owner of Ship**
Journals and logs DD BB 8/4	*Cleveland*	16 Dec 1709 – 9 Mar 1709/10	Liverpool – Barbados	B. Blundell+
"	"	23 Apr – 13 June 1710	Barbados – Liverpool	"
"	"	23 Sept – Dec 1710	Liverpool – Barbados	"
"	"	31 Jan – 10 Mar 1710/11	Barbados – Liverpool	"
"		13 July – 18 Oct 1711	Liverpool – Archangel	"
"	*Cleveland*	17 Jan 1711/12 – 29 May 1712	Liverpool – Barbados	"
"	"	29 May – 14 Jul 1712	Barbados – Liverpool	"
"	"	25 Nov 1712 – 27 Jan 1712/13	Liverpool – Barbados	"
"	"	3 Apr – 18 May 1713	Barbados – London	"
"	"	27 June – 9 Oct 1713	London – Archangel – London	"
"	"	16 Jan 1713/14 – 23 June 1714	Liverpool – Barbados – Liverpool	"
Journal DDX 22/68	*Dolphin* Lancaster	10 Apr – 21 Sept 1774	Lancaster – Jamaica – Lancaster	A. Baldwin*+
"	"	20 Jan – 22 Sept 1775	"	"
"	"	27 Jan – 3 Nov 1776	"	"
"	"	21 Jan – 14 Aug 1777	"	"
"	"	16 Dec 1777 – 23 Sept 1778	"	"
Journal DDTs	*Hope* Drogheda	5 Feb – 25 Apr 1859	Cardiff–Nantes–Donegal–Cork	T. Summer Martin+
Log DDTs	*Ann Shepherd*	29 Aug 1862 – 6 Jun 1863	Liverpool – St Petersburg – Dundee – Liverpool – Rabat –Liverpool	W. Thomas* (in part)
Account book DX1926	*Sprightly*	1849–58		J. Rimmer
Access		Apply to: County Archivist, Lancashire Record Office, Sessions House, Lancaster Road, Preston. Opening hours: Mon – Fri 9–5.15; Sat 9–12.		

LANCASTER CENTRAL PUBLIC LIBRARY

Type of Document	Ship's Name Port of Registry	Period Covered	Voyage(s) Made or Port Type of Business	Master of Ship* or Keeper of Record+ Owner of Ship**
Log book MS 5083	*Chatsworth*	Mar–May 1782	Cork–St Kitts	
		Aug–Sept 1782	St Kitts–Lancaster	
		Mar–Apr 1783	Cork–Barbados	
		July–Aug 1783	St Kitts –Lancaster	
		Nov–Dec 1783	Cork – Dominica	
		Apr–June 1784	Dominica –Lancaster	
		Aug–Sept 1784	Cork–Dominica	
		Jan–Feb 1785	Dominica –St Kitts –Lancaster	
		June–July 1785	Cork–Barbados	
		Oct–Nov 1785	Dominica –Lancaster	
" MS 5085	*Liberty*	Aug 1791	Glasson–Memel	J.Townsend+
		Sept–Oct 1791	Memel–Lancaster	
		May 1792	Glasson–Hamburg	
		June–July 1792	Hamburg–St Petersburg	
"		Aug–Oct 1792	Kronstadt –Lancaster	
MS 5084	*William Ashton* Lancaster	3 May 1810–28 Sept 1811	Cork–Santa Cruz Santa Cruz –Lancaster	T. Greenwood*
			St Croix–London –St Croix –Lancaster	T. Dawson*
Journal (copy)	*Gipsy*	29 Nov 1800 –29 Jan 1801	Lancaster –Trinidad	Capt Towers* R. Batty+
Accounts MS 5164	*Adventure*	1794	Antigua	
Account book MS 3731	*Warre*	to 12 Jan 1798	Trinidad–Glasson	B. Overend*
		22 May 1798	Glasson–Cork–Martinique	J. Lott*
"	*Six Sisters*	1799	Lancaster –Trinidad	J. Kelsey*
MS 238	*Lima Packet*	1835–7	Trinidad –Liverpool	M. Cunningham
		1837	"	G. Wheeler*
	Effort	1836	Trinidad –Limerick	Mahoney*

Type of Document	Ship's Name / Port of Registry	Period Covered	Voyage(s) Made or Port / Type of Business	Master of Ship* or Keeper of Record+ Owner of Ship**
Account book MS 238	*Amethyst*	1836–7	Trinidad – Liverpool	J. Taylor*
	Richard	1836–7	„	W. Black-ley*
Articles of Agreement	*Bee* Lancaster	Sept 1782	Lancaster – Barbados St Lucia, etc	R. Gornall*
Articles, Ships	*Fortitude* Lancaster	1807	Kingston, Jamaica – London	R. Freers*
Instrument of protest	*Sisters* Scarborough	Aug–Oct 1831	Archangel – Lancaster	H.F. Sutton*
Notarial book	*Alcyone* Lancaster	1863	Quebec–Glasson	J.R. Mitchell*
	Favorite Fleetwood	1863	Miramichi – Glasson	J. Allen*
„	*Dorka* Porto Re	1864	Sulina–Cork– Glasson	N. Pollich*
„	*Johanna* Memel	1864	Memel–Glasson	F.W. Siebolds*
„	*Mary Blades* Lancaster	1867	Quebec–Lancaster	J. Hogg*
„	*Muscungus* Liverpool	1869	Miramichi – Glasson	J. Adams*
	Star of Hope Liverpool	1864/5	Quebec–Lancaster	T. Reid*
„	*Express* Greenock	1865	Londonderry – Lancaster	J. Wilson*
„	*Kate Fitzgerald* Liverpool	1866	Liverpool – Cameroons	W.H. Robertson*
„	*Margaret* Liverpool	1866	Liverpool–Perce Chaleur Bay	W.H. Walters*
„	*Therese* Pillau	1868	Onega–Glasson	J.H. Palrow*
„	*Mary Sophia* Cardiff	1869	Kronstadt – Lancaster	T. Elliot*
„	*Thornton* Newcastle	1869	Sulina–Falmouth – Lancaster	A. Carmichael
„	*Favorite* Fleetwood	1869	Liverpool – Halifax, NS –Miramichi– Fleetwood	P. Fea*

Type of Document	Ship's Name Port of Registry	Period Covered	Voyage(s) Made or Port Type of Business	Master of Ship* or Keeper of Record+ Owner of Ship**
Notarial book	*Albatross* Liverpool	1869	Miramichi — Fleetwood	T. Davies*
,,	*Blencathra* Liverpool	1869/70	St Johns, NB — Glasson	J. Stewart*
,,	*Patriot Queen* Liverpool	1871	Miramichi — Glasgow	J. Nicoll*
,,	*Ann Stainland* Liverpool	1871	Norway—Fleetwood	T. O'Reilly*
,,	*Fraternitas* Arendal	1872	Sundsvall — Glasson	S. Loddesoll*
,,	*Bruno* Arendal	1873	Lovisa, Finland — Glasson	G. Pederson*
,,	*Alida* Gothenburg	1875	Gothenburg — Glasson	O.H. Hensson*
,,	*Victoria* Arendal	1875	Miramichi — Glasson	J. Solveson
,,	*Accrington Lass* Fleetwood	1876	Belfast — Morecambe	D. Forshaw*
,,	*Vigilant* Banff	1876	Boston — Glasson	T. Nixon*
,,	*Charles Northcote* Norway	1876	Nova Scotia — Glasson	E. Clauson*
,,	*Undaunted* Plymouth	1877	Boulogne — Lancaster	F. Keast*
,,	*Mary Ann* Liverpool	1877	Miramichi — Glasson	J. Newcombe*
,,	*Anna P. Odell* St Andrews New Brunswick	1880	Sackville, NB — Morecambe	R. Outhouse*
,,	*Mersey* Liverpool	1880	Quebec—Glasson	J. Sutherland*
,,	*Olga Eckan* Caernarvon	1881	Gothenburg — Glasson	O. Davies*
,,	*America* Caernarvon	1881	Hamburg — Glasson	H. Williams*
,,	*Axel* Drammen		Dalhousie, NB — Glasson	P. Knudsen*
,,	*Fern* Glasgow	1882	Portrush — Morecambe	A. McLarty*
,,	*Kate* Langesund	1883	Nova Scotia — Glasson	J. Wright*

Type of Document	Ship's Name Port of Registry	Period Covered	Voyage(s) Made or Port Type of Business	Master of Ship*or Keeper of Record+ Owner of Ship**
Notarial book	*Jenny* Laurvig, Norway	1883	Nova Scotia — Glasson	L. Corn- clinsen*
"	*Silistrio* Lancaster	1884	Campbellton, NB — Glasson	D. McPherson*
"	*Jane* Liverpool	1885	Liverpool — Quebec—Glasson	T.England*
"	"	1886	Miramichi — Glasson	"
"	*Bessie* Maitland, NS	1885	Economy, Nova- Scotia—Glasson	J. Mc- Kenzie*
"	*Buda* St Johns, New Brunswick	3 June—22 July 1886	Montreal — Glasson	W.A. Ray*
"	"	27 Oct—5 Dec 1886	Baie St Paul	"
Package book	*Hope*	27 Sept—8 Oct 1791	Liverpool — Guernsey — Cameroons slaving	Capt T. Collins*
Papers, various, ie sale of ship MS 5165	*Tom*	Feb 1794	Africa — Barbados slaving	Capt T. Collins*
Access	Apply to: City Librarian, Lancaster Central Library, Market Square, Lancaster. Opening hours: Mon, Tue, Thur & Fri 9—7, Wed 9—1, Sat 9—5.			

LEEDS CITY ARCHIVES

Business copies TN/EAI/1		c1592—1629	Shipowning	Sir A. Ingram & Son
	Note: Includes sale of share in voyage to America of Sir W. Raleigh, 1617.			

Type of Document / Port of Registry	Ship's Name	Period Covered	Voyage(s) Made or Port / Type of Business	Master of Ship*or Keeper of Record+ Owner of Ship**
Bills of sale TN/EA6	various vessels Scarborough	1689–99		
Letters GA/Z41		1853–67	England — Australia	

Note: By an emigrant who describes voyage.

Access   Apply to: Archivist, Sheepscar Library, Chapelton Road, Leeds 7.

Opening hours: Mon — Fri, 9–12.30, 2–5.30 (until 8.30 by arrangement) Sat 9–12.30.

LEEDS UNIVERSITY LIBRARY (BROTHERTON LIBRARY)

Type of Document	Ship's Name	Period Covered	Voyage(s) Made or Port	Master of Ship etc.
Journal MS Trv.q1 [ABS]	*America*	31 Dec 1694–29 Oct 1696	Gravesend — Spain	A. Spencer*

Note: Naval victualler's pinnace

Type of Document	Ship's Name	Period Covered	Voyage(s) Made or Port	Master of Ship etc.
Letter MS Trv.1 [APT]		9 July 1711–17 Oct 1715	Eastern Mediterranean	G. Aptall+

Access   Apply to: University Librarian, Brotherton Library, University of Leeds, Leeds 2, Yorks.

Opening hours: Mon — Fri 9–9 (July–Sept 9–5) Sat 9–1.

LEICESTER ARCHIVES

Type of Document	Ship's Name	Period Covered	Voyage(s) Made or Port	Master of Ship etc.
Log 15'1860	*Sea Horse*	9 Nov 1767 — 21 Sept 1769	Gravesend — China	E India Co**

Access   Apply to: Keeper of Archives, Dept of Archives, Leicester Museums & Art Gallery, New Walk, Leicester.

Opening hours: Mon — Fri 10–12.45, 2.15–5, Sat 10–12.

LINCOLNSHIRE ARCHIVES OFFICE

Type of Document	Ship's Name / Port of Registry	Period Covered	Voyage(s) Made or Port / Type of Business	Master of Ship* or Keeper of Record+ Owner of Ship**
Logs Brace 22/ 1/5	*Odin* *Colombo* *Virago* Hull	7–13 Oct 1870 March 1876 1876	Hull – New York	B. Whiteing*
Brace 22/ 3/2	*Sappho* *Hilda* *Southella*	1876 Oct 1876 8 Jan–16 Apr 1878	Hull – Trieste Hull – Kronstadt Hull – Alexandria	
Diary Brace 22/ 3/1	*Virago* Hull	1875	Hull – New York	B. Whiteing*
Account books Brace 22/ 3/3		1876–92		,,

Access   Apply to: Archivist, Lincolnshire Archives Office, The Castle, Lincoln.

Opening hours: Mon – Fri 10–5 (by arrangement during lunch hours); Sat 10–1; advance notice of intended visits is requested.

LIVERPOOL PUBLIC LIBRARIES

Logs	*Ranger* *Enterprise*) *Lotte*) *Fortune*) *Elizabeth* *Garland* *Jumna* Liverpool	1789–90 1793–1811 1815 1833 1833–5	slaving ,, to Miramichi Liverpool – Calcutta – Canton
Journals	*Bloom*) *Pine*) *William*)	1779–88	slaving
Accounts	*Sally* *Ellen* *Enterprise*) *Lotte*) *Fortune*)	1794 1793–1811	To Tortola slaving
Articles of agreement	*Enterprise*	c1796	slaving

Access   Apply to: City Librarian, Liverpool Public Libraries, William Brown Street, Liverpool 3.

Opening hours: Mon – Fri 9–9; Sat 9–5.

Note: This Library also contains the records of the Inman Steamship Co Ltd (qv)

LIVERPOOL UNIVERSITY LIBRARY

Type of Document	Ship's Name	Period Covered	Voyage(s) Made or Port	Master of Ship* or Keeper of Record+ Owner of Ship**
	Port of Registry		Type of Business	
Account books G83931	*Harlequin*	1782–4	Gold Coast, Jamaica	J. Fayrer* Parke & Heywood**
,, G83932	*Madam-pookata*	1783	Angola, Tortola	C. Wilson* Leyland Penny**
,, G83933	*Golden Age*	1783–5	Gold Coast, Jamaica	J. Fayrer* Parke & Heywood**
,, G83934	*Spitfire*	1795–1816	Angola, Grenada	W. Young* T. Leyland**
,, G83935	*Earl of Liverpool*	1797–8	Nigeria, Jamaica	G. Bernard* R. Bullin**
,, G83936	,,	1798–9	,,	G. Bernard* T. Leyland**
,, G83937	,,	1799–1800	Angola, Jamaica	C. Watt* T. Leyland**
,, G83938	*Enterprize*	1806–7	Nigeria, Jamaica	C. Lawson* T. Leyland**

Access   Apply to: Curator of special collections, Library, University of Liverpool, Liverpool 3.

Opening hours: Weekdays 9–5.

MERIONETH COUNTY RECORD OFFICE

Journal M/1/302	*Factor of Barmouth*	Apr–Nov 18, 1816	London–Cape Coast	Price* J. Crool+
Accounts M/1/174	Various Cardigan Bay coasters	1806–8		
Disburse-ment book M/GWO(i)	*Unity*	1781–98	Coastal trade	R. Edwards*
M/GWO(22) (ii)	*Jane Brown*	1840–52	,,	R. Edwards*

Access   Apply to: County Archivist, Merioneth County Record Office, County Offices, Lombard Street, Dolgellau, Merioneth.

Opening hours: Mon, Tues 9–1, 2–5.30; Wed – Fri 9–1, 2–5.

MONMOUTHSHIRE COUNTY RECORD OFFICE

Type of Document	Ship's Name	Period Covered	Voyage(s) Made or Port	Master of Ship* or Keeper of Record+ Owner of Ship**
	Port of Registry		Type of Business	

General information	The archive possesses two related types of document: (a) personal accounts of voyages by members of the Rolls family, 1846–88, mostly in European waters; (b) dates of four yachts maintained by the Rolls family, 1844–1913 (purchase and sale), by books for trips in British and European waters and papers relating to various yacht clubs.
Access	Apply to: County Archivist, Monmouthshire County Record Office, County Hall, Newport, Mon. Opening hours: Mon – Fri, 10–1, 2–5.

NEWCASTLE-UPON-TYNE CITY ARCHIVES

See	Tyne-Tees Shipping Co		

NORFOLK AND NORWICH RECORD OFFICE

Type of Document	Ship's Name / Port of Registry	Period Covered	Voyage(s) Made or Port / Type of Business	Master of Ship* / Keeper of Record+ / Owner of Ship**
Logs NRS2439 11 E 1	*John Baker*	23 Dec 1826 – 18 Mar 1827	Hamburg – Lynn	T. Cook* J. Aires+
Letter bks (6) BLX11f		1826–58		Bagge of** Lynn
Accounts BLXb	*Exchange* Lynn	1791–2	Coaster to Pillau	G. Boothby*
BLX(25)	*Chance* Lynn	1800–5	Coastal	
BL1Xa	*Brilliant* Lynn	1835–6	Lynn – NE Coast	
BLXc	”	1836	”	G. Russell*
BLX11K	*Elizabeth* Lynn	1854–9	”	?G. Peeps*
BLX11c		1824–36		Bagge** of Lynn
BL11e		1833–59 (summary)		”

Type of Document	Ship's Name Port of Registry	Period Covered	Voyage(s) Made or Port Type of Business	Master of Ship* or Keeper of Record+ Owner of Ship**
Bills of Sale BL1Vb	*Two Sisters Experiment* Lynn	1774		
"	*Eclipse* Sunderland	1783		
BLV1b(1)	*Princess Royal* Lynn	1797		
BLX(42)	*Favourite Good Intent Transfer Lincoln*	18th–19th centuries		
Charter parties BLV1a (X111)	*Providence*	1785	Lynn – Lisbon Wheat	R. Cubitt*
BLV111c	*Kitty*	1820	Yarmouth – Dunkirk – Lynn oil cakes	T. Shephard*
Measure bills BLV1b(11)	*Stradsett* Lynn	1796–8		M.Luckelii* R. Hunter*
BLV1a(1)	"	1806		J. Armes*
Receipts for shares BLV1a(1)	*Experiment Archangel* Lynn	1774–5	Greenland fishery	
Papers BL1Xd	*Friendship* Lynn	c1775–1824		
BL1Xd	*Prudence Alexander* Lynn	1777–91		J. Bouch*
BLX1a (X111)	Various	c1780–6		W. & T. Bagge**
BLX11K		1852–71		"

(Register of coal shipments)

Access	Apply to: City & County Archivist, Central Library, Norwich NOR 57E
	Opening hours: Mon – Fri 9–5, Sat 9–12.

UNIVERSITY OF NOTTINGHAM LIBRARY

Type of Document	Ship's Name Port of Registry	Period Covered	Voyage(s) Made or Port Type of Business	Master of Ship* or Keeper of Record+ Owner of Ship**
General information	The documents below may be found in the following collections: Middleton mss (Mi); Mellish mss (Me); Drury Lane (Dr); Bond (Bd).			
Journal Mi x 1/66		1 Sept 1612– 13 May 1613	Newfoundland Coast	

Note: Under ref Mi x 1/–66 papers concerning establishment of colony at Cupers Cove, Conception Bay, Newfoundland, 1620–1631.

Type of Document	Ship's Name	Period Covered	Voyage(s) Made or Port	Master / Owner
Me 182-121	*Hope*	5 Dec 1794	Oporto – to capture by French	Capt J. Goodridge*
Bills of lading Dr E 42	*Mont Horne*	1773–7	From Grenada	R. Smith*
	Two Friends British			T. Newland*
	Queen Arundel			G. Ansell* J. Mann*
" Bd 102	*Adventure Speculation*	1801, 1806	to Berbice (Lancaster Plantation)	A.J. Thompson* W. Lynas*
	Sun			J.R. Strayan
Wages acquittances for Mi 0 16	*George* Lyme	6 July 1572	To Fuenterrabia	
	James Ilcombe, Plymouth *John Evangelist*			T. Brod*
Letters Me 151-90		May 1675 – July 1698		

Note: concerning Levant Co trade; includes list of cargoes of 7 ships leaving 'Scanderoone' for London, 26 May 1696

Access   Apply to: Keeper of MSS, University of Nottingham Library, Nottingham.

Opening hours: Mon – Fri 9–5, Sat 9–12.30.

PLYMOUTH CITY LIBRARY

Type of Document	Ship's Name Port of Registry	Period Covered	Voyage(s) Made or Port Type of Business	Master of Ship* or Keeper of Record+ Owner of Ship**
Journal Acc 216		1830	Madagascar	Capt J. Lyons+
,, Acc 298	Toxteth	1894—5		Capt R. Dale+
Account book Acc 298	Tredinnick	1921—3		,,
Accounts, Wages Acc 298	,,	1923		,,

Access Apply to: City Librarian, City of Plymouth Public Libraries, Tavistock Road, Plymouth.

Opening hours: Mon — Fri 9.30—5.30; Sat 9.30—12.

SHEFFIELD CITY LIBRARIES

Bills of Lading, Agreements and Correspondence 60550	Roan Packet Don Philip	1750—4	London — West Africa — West Indies — S. Carolina—London (slaving)	B.Spencer (in part)**
	Catherine	1752—4		
	General Wall	1754—5		
	Cannon Hall	1755—6		
	Endeavour	1756		
	Mermaid	1758		
Insurance policies 60551		1754—8		B.Spencer+

Access Apply to: City Librarian, Dept of Local History and Archives, Sheffield City Archives, Surrey Street, Sheffield 1.

Opening hours: Mon — Sat 10—5.30.

SOMERSET RECORD OFFICE

General information The archive holds two principal collections of shipping documents: (a) Carew of Crowcombe MSS (DD/TB) and (b) Dickinson of Kingwestern MSS (DD/DN) for which see also *A guide to Manuscripts Relating to America in Great Britain and Ireland* (1961), 405 6.

Type of Document	Ship's Name Port of Registry	Period Covered	Voyage(s) Made or Port Type of Business	Master of Ship* or Keeper of Record+ Owner of Ship**
Journal DD/TB	*Bombay Merchant*	May 1698 – Jan 1699 Apr 1700 – Apr 1701	Bombay—Calcutta —Acheen	Capt G. Smythes*+
"	*Blessing*	May 1702 – Feb 1703	Bombay—Chusan Bombay – Amoy – Malacca	" "
Journal (copy)	[small junk]	Oct–Nov 1699	Amoy—Chusan— Quemoy	W. Hill+
Accounts DD/DN	*Parham* Bristol	1729–46	England—Carolina – Lisbon Baltic—Hamburg —Cork—England	E. Will-iams* N. Allo-way*
" DD/DN	*Sea Flower*	1739–42	Baltic	H. Atwell*
Access	Apply to: County Archivist, Somerset Record Office, Obridge Road, Taunton, Somerset. Opening hours: Mon – Fri, 9.15–1, 2.15–5.15; Sat 9.15–12.15.			

WILLIAM SALT LIBRARY, STAFFORD

Log & Journal HM Drake-ford 4	*Falmouth*	1719–21		Capt Wade* R. Drake-ford+
Journal (copy) SMS 398	*Eagle*	1624–5	England – Surat – England	East India Co** J. Weddell* W. Mynors+
Access	Apply to: Librarian, William Salt Library, 19 Eastgate Street, Stafford. Opening hours: Tue–Sat 10–1, 2–5, Mon by arrangement at Staffordshire Record Office, County Buildings, Eastgate Street, Stafford.			

EAST SUSSEX RECORD OFFICE

Account Book Frewer MS	*Teneriffe* London?	1647–53	Canary Islands	R. New-man*
Addl MS 4881	not known Rye?	c1710–14	Yarmouth – London	D. Lil-*+ bourne?
Access	Apply to: County Archivist, Pelham House, Lewes. Opening hours: Mon – Fri 9–12.30, 1.30–5.			

WEST SUSSEX RECORD OFFICE

Type of Document	Ship's Name	Period Covered	Voyage(s) Made or Port	Master of Ship* or Keeper of Record+ Owner of Ship**
	Port of Registry		Type of Business	
Log Add Ms 2256	*Lord Eldon*	Aug 1810 – Oct 1810 Mar–Apr 1811 Oct–Nov 1811 May–July 1812	England – Bombay Bombay–Batavia Batavia–Bombay Bombay–St Helena	R. Halsted+
Access	Apply to: County Archivist, West Sussex Record Office, County Hall, Chichester, Sussex. Opening hours: Mon – Fri 9.15–1, 2–5.			

UNIVERSITY COLLEGE LONDON

Logs (photo)	*Britannia Speedy*	1791–6	Whaling	
Access	Apply to: Librarian, University College London, Gower Street, London WC 1 Opening hours: Mon – Fri 9.30 Sat 9.30–12.30 (term only)			

NATIONAL LIBRARY OF WALES

Logs Glansev- em MS 14256	*Turnpenny Blewett*	27 Nov 1751 – 21 May 1752	Portugal	N. Simpson+
do 14259	*Edward*	24 Oct – 2 Dec 1767	New York – England	T. Miller*
NLW MS 17817	*Fortune*	Oct 1774 – Apr 1775	Sumatra – Bengal and back	
NLW MS 17818	*Resolution*	Feb 1780 – Dec 1782	India – East Indies	
NLW MS 10833	*York*	3 Dec 1785 – 29 Mar 1787	Gravesend – China and back	W. Huddart*
NLW MS 15462	*Liberty*	18 July 1804 – 17 May 1806	London – Surinam and back	
NLWMS 15463	*Lord Nelson*	12 Dec 1810 – 31 Dec 1812	London to Mediterranean	
NLW MS 11518	*Robert Small*	30 July 1840 – 1 Mar 1841	London to Calcutta	D. Evans+

Type of Document	Ship's Name / Port of Registry	Period Covered	Voyage(s) Made or Port / Type of Business	Master of Ship* or Keeper of Record+ Owner of Ship**
NLW MS 16585	*Britannia*	9 June 1841 – 29 Mar 1844	England to Solva	H. Williams+
NLW MS 17293	*Magellan*	9 Sept 1854 – 9 Dec 1856	London – Australia (2 voyages)	T. Jones+
NLW MS 17294	*Joseph Sanderson; MacVicar*	17 Feb – 19 June 1854 Nov 1857	Calcutta – Liverpool London – New Zealand	J. Chester
	General Windham	17 May – 12 Sept 1858	Sydney – London	
NLW MS 17295	*Maia*	30 May – 9 Aug 1859	Liverpool to Cape	T. Jones*
		9 Sept 1859 – 3 May 1860	East London – Mauritius – Liverpool	,,
		28 July 1860 – 25 Mar 1861	Liverpool – Montevideo – Hull	,,
	Celestial	19 June – 27 Oct 1861	Liverpool – Shanghai	,,
		27 Dec 1861 23 Apr 1862	Shanghai – London	,,
		30 May – 30 June 1862	London – Shanghai	,,
NLW MS 6651	*Lunaria*	1860–1	Antwerp – Montevideo	
NLW MS 615	*Viscount Sandon*	1860–1	Newcastle – Hong Kong – Rangoon – Liverpool	E. Hughes*
NLW MS 17296	not known	14 Feb 1867 – 24 May 1868	Gravesend – Bombay and back	
NLW MS 1469-70	*Alexandra*	1868–9	Liverpool – Calcutta and back (2 voyages)	D. Jones+
NLW MS 16641	*Oswingo*	8 Aug – 25 Dec 1876	Manila – New York – Glasgow	T. Hughes?+
NLW MS 10361	*Highland Laird*	1904–5	Liverpool – R Plate	J.H. Evans+

Type of Document	Ship's Name	Period Covered	Voyage(s) Made or Port	Master of Ship* or Keeper of Record+ Owner of Ship**
	Port of Registry		Type of Business	
NLW MS 18613	*Solway Prince*	20 Oct 1906 — 3 Jan 1907	Irish Sea trade	
NLW MS 16588	*Kolyma*	23 June — 11 Nov 1923	England — Baltic	
Accounts NLW MS 18608	*Sincerity* Aberdovey	1820—5		R. Lewis*
NLW MS 12107	*Economy*	1829—30		W. Watkins*
NLW MS 18395	*Catherine* Newquay	1839—48		
NLW MS 16589	*Agenoria*	1839	Cardiff — Waterford	
NLW MS 18609	*Catherine Hodges* Aberdovey	1844—51		R. Lewis*
NLW MS 12108	*William* Portmadoc	1844—54		H. Watkins* R. Hughes* J. Roberts*
NLW MS 16586	*Hope*	1847—52		
NLW MS 12105	*Star* Pwllheli *William* Portmadoc	1851—9		W. Parry* R. Owen* W. Williams* O. Williams*
NLW MS 16224	*Hope*	1853—9		J. Jenkins* J. Jones* J. Thomas* M. Williams** D. Jenkins**
NLW MS 12506	*New Valiant* Portmadoc	1849—62		G. Griffiths*
NLW MS 18936	*Sylph*	1873—6		
Diary NLW MS 18176	*Mimosa*	19 Apr — 27 July 1863 (in Welsh)	Liverpool — Patagonia	J.S. Jones+
NLW MS 17930		1881—2	Sydney — London — San Francisco — Cork	A.K. Jones+

141 NATIONAL LIBRARY OF WALES/WILTSHIRE RECORD OFFICE

Type of Document	Ship's Name Port of Registry	Period Covered	Voyage(s) Made or Port Type of Business	Master of Ship* or Keeper of Record+ Owner of Ship**
NLW MS 17239	*Paris*	Sep 25 — 4 Oct 1893	New York — Southampton	
Freight book NLW MS 18611	*Catherine Hodges*	1842—56		R. Lewis*
NLW MS 18612	*Italian Hero* Aberystwyth	1876—9		R.R. Lewis*
Bills of Lading NLW MS 17301	*Caroline Coventry*	1867		T. Jones*
Various NLWMS 17288	"	May 1864		
Engineer book NLW MS 16587	*Tyninghame* Cardiff	1914—15		T. Williams+
Insurance cert NLW MS 12511	*Five Sisters*	8 Feb 1830	Conway — Swansea copper one	
Sight bk NLWMS 11520	*Mermaid*	1843—5		D.W. Evans+
Various NLW MS 10294	*The Friends* Milford	1810—14		R. Richards*

Access Apply to: Keeper of MSS, National Library of Wales, Aberystwyth.
Opening hours: Mon — Fri 9.30—6, Sat 9—5.

WILTSHIRE RECORD OFFICE

Account Book 332/288	*Edgecote*	1755—7	Bombay — London, Surat, Mocha	J. Pearse* East India Co**

Access Apply to: County Archivist, Wiltshire Record Office, County Hall, Trowbridge, Wilts.

Opening hours: Mon 8.50—5.50, Tues — Fri 8.50—5.20.

WORCESTERSHIRE COUNTY RECORD OFFICE

Type of Document	Ship's Name	Period Covered	Voyage(s) Made or Port	Master of Ship* or Keeper of Record
	Port of Registry		Type of Business	Owner of Ship**
Account Book b705: 24/980		1774–5	West Indies: slaves, gunpowder, cloth, rum, etc	
Account Insurance policies 705:288/3	*Caradog*	1888–1910		F.S. Brooke*

Access	Apply to: County Archivist, Worcestershire Record Office, Shire Hall, Worcester.
	Opening hours: Mon – Fri 9–12.45, 2–5.